Testimonials

"Chris Hatfield's coaching was genuinely a game-changer for my mental health and work performance. Naturally, at the start of a job, there is a lot of pressure to hit targets and get the hang of things. Over the past couple of years, the tools in this book have made such a huge difference for me. Now I'm rarely anxious or burnt out, and I feel like I have a much better relationship with my work."

Nikolai Veresinin
Customer Success Manager

"I want to say a HUGE thank you to Chris Hatfield for all his help over the past few months. I signed up for a Sales Psyche course with Chris after essentially being in a career 'hole.' In a world of targets and pressure, I was struggling to keep my head above water and had allowed stress to get the better of me. These tools provided practical, tangible tasks that I could apply to these stressful moments. I have done a complete 180 mentally and my motivation is on an upward trend. This was a life raft for me."

Michelle Cleaver
Account Executive

"The tools that Chris shares in his coaching sessions not only helped me with my own mindset and how I approach work and personal challenges, but I know they'll make me a better leader for years to come in how I support my team. My learning? Don't wait until you're struggling or hit a setback to work on your mindset. Investing in yourself proactively will pay off!"

Natasha Evans
Head of Customer Success

"Working with Chris has been one of the best personal investments I have made in my career. The insights and protocols I've learnt have proven to be valuable not just within my professional life, but also in life more generally. As a result, I have seen a huge improvement in my levels of motivation, resilience and performance through the tools Chris provided."

Ed Cooke
US Sales Manager

"Despite having more than seven years' experience in recruitment, I suffered massively from imposter syndrome, negative self-talk and a lack of confidence in my own ability, which I hid from others. Since using the tools provided by Chris, which you'll find in this book, I am now able to accept and understand my own emotions and thoughts, as well as having a much better understanding of how other people may be feeling. I have learnt coping mechanisms to rationalise my thoughts when I am feeling overwhelmed, anxious or just generally doubting myself."

Chloe White
Senior Recruitment Consultant

"I've worked with Chris for over two years and the sessions have been impactful for me as a Sales Professional. Chris has helped me identify areas for improvement and he's taught me strategies that help me manage the rollercoaster of Sales.

One of the biggest takeaways has been learning how to reframe anxiety so that it doesn't control me. In the past, my anxiety would cause me to over-prepare for calls and then over-work, which lead to burnout. Once I was suffering from burnout, I started my sessions with Chris and he got me back on track. I started implementing his suggestions with time blocks using upper and lower boundaries, and my productivity, confidence and sales results improved as well. Thank you Chris!"

Rebecca Manias
Enterprise Account Manager

"In sales, limiting beliefs can be your worst enemy. As a gay man in a senior global role, I've battled some deep-rooted doubts. Chris doesn't promise to erase negativity, but has helped me acknowledge and reframe it. I feel I'm doing the best work of my career because I'm having more fun and massively enjoying the journey. I use many of the techniques Chris taught daily – not just for sales but for life."

Dan Cox
Global Account Director

"The coaching has been instrumental not only in enhancing my coaching abilities, but also in supporting my mental health. It has helped me recognise and address my own limitations, allowing me to improve as a manager, coach, and leader, who has over 13 years of experience in recruitment.

The various techniques I learned have been incredibly beneficial, not just for my personal growth but also in improving the performance of my team. I've seen significant positive changes both in myself and in my team members. With these tools, Chris delves deeply into various communication techniques and methods with structure and clarity, providing a comprehensive approach that is delivered exceptionally well."

Adam Garvey
Division Manager

"Chris's coaching has helped me grow both as a sales professional and personally. Over the last few years I have struggled with thinking in ways that were not helpful - my irrational brain had become dominant and was beginning to stand in the way of my progression. Chris has helped me engage my rational brain and think through situations with a different perspective, which has elevated my performance in sales as well as my well being outside of the workplace. Through the use of various simple tools, pattern interruption, and building habits, I now approach situations with a different mindset. I would encourage anyone who feels like they're caught in a similar pattern to speak to Chris to gain this fresh perspective so you feel like you have a clear path forward again."

Oliver
Enterprise Account Manager

Published by
LID Publishing
An imprint of LID Business Media Ltd.
LABS House, 15-19 Bloomsbury Way,
London, WC1A 2TH, UK

info@lidpublishing.com
www.lidpublishing.com

A member of:

BPR ✦
businesspublishersroundtable.com

© Chris Hatfield, 2024
© LID Business Media Limited, 2024
Reprinted in 2025

Printed and bound in Great Britain by Halstan Ltd
ISBN: 978-1-915951-61-8
ISBN: 978-1-915951-62-5 (ebook)

Cover and page design: Caroline Li

Chris Hatfield

Sales Psyche

A Guide to
Mastering a **Healthy &
High-Performing Mind**

MADRID | MEXICO CITY | LONDON
BUENOS AIRES | BOGOTA | SHANGHAI

Contents

Part C
Unlocking the True Meanings of Motivation
106

Part D
Learning From the Setbacks in Sales
154

Part E

Unleashing Your Inner Sales Champion

206

Part F

Sustaining Consistency by Managing
& Protecting Your Energy

270

Part G
Finding Your Off Switch to Recharge in Sales
322

ACKNOWLEDGEMENTS & DEDICATIONS

First, to those who've contributed to this guide, I'm sure your stories and vulnerability about past challenges will resonate with and inspire many people reading this.

To those I've coached over the last nine years, thank you for being willing to share your stories of transformation here. In doing so, you're helping people recognise that they're not alone in how they're thinking or feeling.

I'd also like to thank LID Publishing for providing me with the platform to share this guide and the key messages within, to support the world of salespeople. Thanks also to The Book Edit team (Emily & Holly) for your initial support in helping me craft and format this guide.

Introduction

In the relentless world of sales, where targets loom large, stress is a constant companion and the unexpected is never far away, your mind and wellbeing can take a battering. No matter how much knowledge you have about your product or how you present it, if you can't manage and take care of your mind, you'll be fighting a constant, losing battle.

First of all, I'm here to tell you that you're not alone in this.

A Gartner survey found that 89% of salespeople feel burned out from work,[1] and this elephant in the room is not only impacting your mindset, but often your actual sales performance. Studies collected in corporate training consultant Shawn Achor's book, *The Happiness Advantage*, have shown that sales professionals with greater happiness and a sense of wellbeing outperform their counterparts by 37% in revenue generation and are 31% more productive.[2]

Yet, despite this very evident need to take care of your perspective and disposition for the sake of your mental health and performance, working on this is often a very reactive thing in sales. Many people seem to wait until they feel unmotivated, burnt out, underperforming or thinking of leaving their role altogether before they start paying attention to it.

When you do go looking for resources to help, you turn to sales books or courses, but these often focus on skills development, with very little on how to work on your mindset or overall wellbeing. They may teach you how to handle your prospects' objections, but what about your own internal objections, when you're immersed in your own self-talk about what could go wrong and why you won't be successful?

They'll give you tips on time management, but not about how to manage your energy during that time and prevent burnout. You may be told what the perfect cold call or sales cycle looks like, but not how to handle self-doubt or the knockbacks that may come from it.

So, you may then think, let's turn to general-purpose books on wellbeing and mindset. But, for the most part, they're written by those outside the world of sales, who haven't felt what you've felt. They haven't had to start from scratch again, or faced new and unexpected challenges each and every day. You're then required to do the hard work of translating how the learnings apply to your sales role.

You may ask others for advice, and hear comments like, 'Just have a positive mindset,' or 'Just be confident.' But these feel-good catchphrases lack substance, and treat your disposition as if it were a switch you can simply flick on and change. This often leaves you feeling even more alone and not knowing what to do. The world of sales has evolved, and it's about time there were more resources to reflect this and address the most important tool at your disposal: your mind.

These are some of the many reasons why I wrote *Sales Psyche*. This guide bridges the gap between understanding how to improve your sales performance alongside your mindset and wellbeing. It dives into the essential mental and emotional tools that are often overlooked in sales, but are crucial for unlocking your full potential.

This isn't your typical resource. It's not a book filled with tons of theory or endless insights that lack suggested ways of applying them. It's an interactive guide detailing 30+ activities you can start instantly applying to your day-to-day sales role and everyday life. It offers insights and tools that go way beyond 'Just have a positive mindset' or 'Be resilient.'

I delve deep into strategies and insights that will empower you to conquer the stresses and uncertainties inherent in sales. This guide will also help you overcome the confidence-draining challenges of self-comparison with others, and teach you how to become your own greatest advocate.

It will support you in unlocking the often-neglected realm of energy management, with tools to prevent or handle burnout and maintain a healthy work-life balance, to consistently hit and exceed your sales targets.

I'll also help you conquer limiting beliefs and reframe emotions in high-pressure sales situations. This guide equips you with the mindset and tools you need to take care of yourself and thrive in both your personal life and your sales performance.

It not only addresses the many elephants in the world of sales, but also teaches you how to understand, overcome and even utilise them.

Like so many other salespeople, I was heavily stressed and consumed with anxiety when I began my sales career. I was selling door-to-door, working on 100% commission.

When I got anxious about hitting my targets, I became frustrated with myself, which only made things worse. I gradually started applying the sports coaching methods I'd learnt at university to my sales work and saw my performance transformed.

Overcoming these challenges led me to found my own company, Sales Psyche, during the COVID-19 pandemic in 2020. Since then, I've worked with some of the highest-performing multinational companies and individuals in the world, including Meta, Google, Shopify, Snowflake and Salesforce, to name a few.

The insights and tools shared in this guide are not simply nice ideas that sound good on paper, or complex hypotheses wrapped up in theory. They're based on real-life situations and experiences I've worked through and learnt from the last 15+ years, and I used to train and coach thousands of individuals to develop their mindset and emotional intelligence. These tools have been road-tested in some of the world's most influential, high-pressure workplaces.

But this guide isn't just filled with my knowledge and experience. It also contains insights from two dozen thought leaders, sharing their own personal challenges in life and sales, what they did to deal with them and the results they've seen. And there will be stories of adversity from people I've coached and trained, and how they overcame their hurdles.

Focusing on your mindset isn't just about feeling better within yourself, but also elevating your performance. By embracing the insights and tools in this guide you'll be able to cultivate a resilient mindset and use it to drive a strong, sustainable sales performance. Imagine facing each day equipped with the emotional intelligence and tools needed to navigate even the most challenging situations.

So, what can I promise you from reading this book? First, you'll finish it feeling empowered, more self-aware and focused on how to utilise your mind to its full potential in your sales role. You'll feel equipped to build more sustainable and consistent approaches to your sales career that will boost your performance, but not at the expense of your life outside work.

You'll also recognise that you're not alone in what you're thinking or feeling, and how going through these experiences can be one of the best ways to learn from and overcome them. This book will not only make you a better seller or manager, but it will also support you in becoming the best version of yourself.

Don't wait for a bad quarter, low motivation or contemplating quitting before committing yourself to reading and internalising this guide. Take control of your situation, here and now. It's never too late. Wherever you are in your journey, instead of thinking, 'I should have started this sooner,' tell yourself, 'I'm starting this sooner than I could have.'

If you want to gain a better understanding of how to build a healthy, high-performing mindset, which contributes to consistent, sustainable sales success, this book is for you. I'm confident your future self will thank you for reading it in the years to come.

How to best use this guide

Before moving ahead, I want to share some tips on how to get most out of this guide. They'll ensure that you can embody these insights and tools, and create the right habits to elevate your sales performance and maintain a healthy mindset.

1. Be proactive with the tools before you need them.

The more proactive you are, the less reactive you'll need to be. When you incorporate these tools into your habits and routines, you'll be far more likely to call upon them when you do need them. Just as with presenting your product or handling objections, practice them ahead of time to embed them into your thought process and approach.

2. Be patient with yourself when working on these areas.

Some will come easier than others, but recognise the value of the ones that don't. It's like when you started cold calling or trying to close deals; the more you do it, the more familiar it becomes. Just as those achy muscles after a good run or workout are a sign of progress, it will pay to be persistent and stay consistent with practising them.

3. Use this guide like a playlist.

Think of this guide like your go-to playlist. Just as you return to your favorite tracks to shift your mood or find inspiration, you can revisit this guide whenever you need a quick refresher on how to handle situations as they unfold. While working through the guide in order will give you the best experience, feel free to skip around if something specific is on your mind.

You will find a section at the end of the guide called 'The Playbook.' It provides a list of specific scenarios and guidance on which tools you can use to work on them. This is a great resource to refer to when faced with new situations, and one managers can also benefit from, by using them in 1:1 sessions or team training.

4. Create anchor reminders.

Creating visual reminders (anchors) of specific tools and tips can further support you in developing your craft. Here are some suggestions for this:

> Use post-it notes, with a visual icon to remind you of the tools, and stick them somewhere visible.

> Put reminders in your calendar to prompt you at certain times.

> Tell a colleague, close friend, partner or manager about something you're working on, and ask them to regularly check in with you on it.

5. Access exercise worksheets online.

You'll find 30+ practical exercises in this guide and whilst there is space to make notes for each, you can find all the exercise worksheets online, using the QR code here.

Doing the above will help ensure that you get full use out of this guide.

And so, without further ado, let's get started.

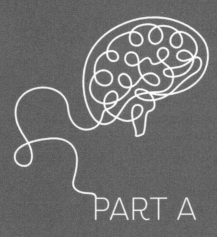

Mastering Your Mind for Peak Sales Performance

I've worked with hundreds of salespeople and leaders, with various levels of experience and success, over the past few years. One of the most consistent themes that comes up as a challenge for them is understanding and managing their mindset.

You are going to be with yourself for the rest of your life, so it's important to understand and build a healthy relationship with your internal voice – your self-talk.

In this first part of the guide we'll focus first on 'limiting beliefs' and how these internal objections can often be our biggest blocker in being successful in sales and taking care of our mindset.

You'll gain tools to reframe or challenge these beliefs, build frameworks to navigate them when they occur, and become more conscious of building a healthier relationship with your self-talk. Along the way, we'll look at why 'luck' is an unhelpful term to use in sales, or get too focused on, and how reframing your comfort zone can change the way you embrace new challenges and change, which are everyday occurrences in sales.

After reading this first part, you'll have all the tools you need to master your mindset, become more conscious of your self-talk, and help ensure that it's working with you, not constantly doubting or challenging you.

CHAPTER 1

Rewiring Your Sales Beliefs for Success

I want to start by sharing a story with you. There was a man who travelled the world, and during his excursions he visited India. One day, while walking through a field crowded with people, he noticed a large group of elephants standing motionless. Intrigued, he wondered why these enormous animals weren't moving.

Upon closer observation, he discovered that each elephant had a rope tied around one of its ankles, looped around a peg planted in the ground. Given their size, he thought that surely they could easily pull the peg out of the ground and run away.

He approached one of the guides who was accompanying the elephants and asked why they weren't trying to pull the pegs out. The guide explained that when the elephants were younger, when moving them between reserves, their handlers would use the same rope and peg to keep them from running away. Initially, when they were small, they would try to pull the rope, but due to their lack of strength, were unable to do so.

Over time, they gradually stopped attempting to free themselves. As fully grown elephants, they had come to accept that they could never break free. Consequently, this small piece of rope and peg held these massive elephants in place, even though it logically had no power to do so.

This piece of rope symbolises the limiting beliefs we can have about ourselves, others and the world around us. The peg is the belief that we will always have these limitations, and we'll never be able to overcome them.

Limiting beliefs can take various forms, and be either directly related to your role or to your own identity and personality. In sales we can be very focused on the objections we face from prospects, but it's critical that we become more aware of our own internal objections, in the form of limiting beliefs.

I was contracted to work with a Software as a Service (SaaS) company on a 30-day programme with their Account Executives (AEs) and Business Development Reps (BDRs). Senior management had been grappling with constant challenges in the team, and attributed this to how employees managed their self-talk, which had eroded their confidence over the years.

To kick off the first workshop, I had them anonymously share their limiting beliefs on Post-it notes. See some examples overleaf. Do they sound familiar to you?

Limiting beliefs related to sales role	Limiting beliefs related to salesperson's identity
I'm not good at cold calling.	I'm not good with saying 'no' to others.
I always struggle speaking with C-level execs.	I can't ever focus on one activity at a time.
I'll never be as knowledgeable as my colleagues when it comes to the product.	I'm always late for things.
If my first few calls go poorly, I always have a bad day.	I'm not good with money and spend my commission on things I don't need.
I won't ever be confident enough to become a manager of a team.	I never seem to do 'enough' to feel satisfied.

These are common limiting beliefs. And when someone asks why we hold onto them, we might respond with, 'That's just the way I am,' or 'A person was once really rude to me on a cold call,' or 'I saw others struggling to engage with that customer.' However, there's a reason these beliefs are lodged in your brain.

Imagine that your mind is like Google. Whatever you type in, it will provide evidence to support it. In sales, it's easy to become fixated on the negatives – all the things that might not go according to plan, why we won't achieve our targets, uncontrollable factors such as market condition, our competitor's offering, or how a prospect reacted to us. The problem with these internal conversations is that they often determine the outcomes. To gain a deeper understanding of our mind and why this occurs, it's necessary to know more about our rational brain and our primal brain.

The Rational Brain

This is the most evolved part of our brain, responsible for complex thinking and knowledge. It is logical, and it can distinguish between the past, present and future. We're highly aware of our thoughts originating from this region (though sometimes we wish we weren't). The rational brain thrives on variety, hence our desire for novelty and new experiences. It is also the part of the brain we use to solve problems when we're faced with questions.

The Primal Brain

This is our prehistoric brain, and it is driven by emotion. It doesn't think rationally and is guided by our feelings. It operates in the present tense, so when you think about an upcoming demo or a tough call from last week, it can make you feel like it's happening right now. That's why we experience anxiety and stress when contemplating such moments.

The primal brain craves familiarity, which explains our inclination to form habits and struggle with change. It also contains the amygdala, our inner smoke alarm, which goes off at the sign of any threat or uncertain change, causing our rational brain to disengage. This is known as amygdala hijack, and is often when you'll find a lot of limiting beliefs and statements showing up.

No matter how good you are at selling, and how extensive the knowledge you possess about your product or industry, if you allow your primal brain to take control and run riot, you won't be able to reach your full potential. I've seen people in every position – well-versed AEs, Account Directors and Sales Leaders, who are great at what they do – crumble as soon as they're hit with stressful, challenging moments.

The aim here is not to stop your primal brain from jumping it, as it has a lot of value to offer. We'll talk about that in a minute. Rather, you need to recognise when it's in the driving seat, and how to kickstart your rational brain to bring more reasoned, logical thinking to the situation.

When we latch onto these limiting beliefs, our brains actively search for evidence to confirm them, strengthening our commitment to those beliefs and values around a situation. This is known as confirmation bias, and our primal brain uses it to avoid us being proved wrong. We hate others proving us wrong, and the same goes for ourselves – our primal brain wants to back us up in every situation.

For example, if we convince ourselves that we'll have a bad day, that a call won't go well or that we won't be able to connect with someone, our brains will look for all the supporting evidence. That could be previous unsuccessful calls, a few demos that didn't go as planned, or even anecdotes from other team members that we haven't actually experienced ourselves.

Another aspect of this that's really important to be aware of is the Nocebo Effect, put forward by the academics Luana Colloca & Damien Finnis.[3] This is where negative expectations can cause a situation to have a more negative effect than it otherwise would. It's the opposite of the Placebo Effect, where positive expectations can lead to a more positive outcome.

For instance, a salesperson might expect prospects to be uninterested in their company's new product, and therefore misinterpret neutral or even positive signals as a negative reaction. A prospect's question might mistakenly be seen as a sign of doubt rather than interest, causing the salesperson to react defensively or pessimistically.

Another example of this might be when you've had a couple of tough cold calls in the morning. You may start to expect that all calls that day will, therefore, also go poorly. This belief can lead to a more timid, cautious approach, which prospects could perceive as lack of enthusiasm or confidence, resulting in a self-fulfilling prophecy of continued negative responses.

We'll come back to the Nocebo Effect a couple of times in this guide, as it can also relate to how you interpret your emotions.

As you can see, if we aren't conscious of our thoughts, we end up playing these limiting beliefs over and over in our heads. This gives them more of a hold over us, affecting our performance, impacting our wellbeing and limiting our potential. To avoid this, one thing we can start working on is looking at how we frame limiting thoughts.

Inspirational Insights

Mark Ash, Chief Revenue Officer (CRO) of Konica Minolta, which manufactures business and industrial imaging products, summarises this nicely:

"Reality is not what happens to you," he told me. "Your perception is what determines your reality."

I met Mark through a networking group that I spoke to a couple of years ago. He attended one of my group course programmes on stress and burnout prevention. He subsequently invited me to work with his sales function (90+ people).

From the moment I met Mark I could tell he was a very reflective person, who really lives by his quote above. He had a big moment in his life where he was able to apply this thinking, when he was cycling in the countryside and was hit from behind by a car going more than 50 mph.

What I appreciated about his approach is that we can't control a lot of what happens to us on a daily basis, but we can always control how we respond and think about what we do next.

Turning Limiting Belief Statements into Questions

Sometimes, reframing limiting beliefs can be an instant solution to overcoming them. We can do this by changing the self-talk statement into a question. We can't use both parts of our brain at once, so when we're in a primal head-space, thinking of these limiting beliefs, reframing them as a question can interrupt the process and engage the rational part of our brain. We can then think of potential solutions that can be acted on, to manage this reframed question.

Now, let's look at some examples from the AEs and BDRs from that SaaS company, with their reframed questions and potential solutions to resolve the question.

Limiting Belief statement	Reframed question	Potential solutions
I'm not good at cold calling.	How can I become more comfortable with cold calling?	• Build more of a routine for it. • Speak to others who are doing well with it. • Work on the way I open the call.
I never seem to do 'enough' to feel satisfied.	What could I have done by the end of this week to feel satisfied?	• 2-4 workouts. • Made at least 150 calls. • Learnt one new thing about my industry from a podcast.
I'll never be as knowledgeable as my colleagues when it comes to the product.	What are 1-2 things I can focus on learning this month to become more knowledgeable about the product?	• Read up on 2-3 case studies on the positive impact it's had for existing customers. • Listen in on one call a week conducted by a colleague I see as having good product knowledge.
If my first few calls are bad at the start of the day, I always have a bad day.	How can I reset myself if I have a few tough calls today?	• Go outside for five minutes to get fresh air. • Speak to a colleague who helps me reset.

You can probably already see a difference in how these reframed questions might make you feel, versus the limiting belief statements. They kickstart your mind and get it working on solving the problem, rather than sitting on it. When limiting beliefs do pop up, simply ask yourself, 'What's the question here?' This can help you to reframe them.

Psyche Success Stories — Arti & The 'Direct' Decision Maker

I was working with Arti, a Sales Development Rep (SDR), who had been in her role for nearly a year in a cybersecurity company. Arti had booked a series of one-on-one coaching sessions with me after realising she was consistently 'her own worst enemy' when it came to selling. She had detected a particular limiting belief that was showing up again and again in her role.

The limiting belief statement she would tell herself each day was, 'I'm not good at speaking with the heads of IT functions, who are short and direct in their communication.' As a result, she found herself scrambling every time one picked up the phone, and even dreading most calls, afraid of encountering one of these individuals. This led to her feeling constantly worried and making fewer calls, which led to missing her sales targets.

When we started working together and examining this limiting belief, Arti began reframing it into a question: 'What can I do to become more comfortable speaking with a head of IT?' She determined that she could shorten her opener and mirror the style of an IT lead. To help with this, she could ask colleagues how they dealt with those prospects.

She queried colleagues on their style and re-crafted her opener, mirroring how the prospects communicated, keeping it tight and punchy. As she put the new approach to use, she quickly began to feel more confident.

As a result, she felt less apprehensive about cold calling these individuals, which meant her call volume became more consistent. And when they did pick up, she knew what to focus on, which led to not only meeting her target, but exceeding it.

Activity A1 –
Reframing Your Limiting Beliefs

Use the table below to note down some of the limiting beliefs that exist for you in your role. Then, jot down how you could reframe each into a question, and note potential solutions you could focus on to reduce the limiting beliefs.

Limiting Belief statement	Reframed question	Potential solutions

Reframing limiting beliefs can be a useful way to tackle them in the moment. Sometimes, though, if they're constantly showing up in the same sort of situation, it's worth digging deeper to better understand when they're occurring and how to manage them.

Your Three Key Takeaways:

1) Be conscious of amygdala hijack — that strong emotional reaction — and how it can cause you to think and behave irrationally.

2) Recognise when confirmation bias may be at play, and how it can influence your thoughts and beliefs.

3) Reframe limiting belief statements into questions, to activate your rational brain.

CHAPTER 2

Noticing and Naming Your Limiting Beliefs

Limiting beliefs may feel ever-present, but they're often amplified or kickstarted by a particular event. That might be a demo you're nervous about doing, a one-on-one with your manager, or a particularly rude prospect. If we don't look to address these limiting beliefs, they'll often lead to negative outcomes. These could include changing a sales process that has historically served you well, losing sleep or feeling more anxious, which can lead to a palpable sense of desperation on your sales calls.

This is often our default thought pattern when it comes to limiting beliefs, but we have the power to change that and avoid those negative outcomes. If we can become more aware of the limiting beliefs and the events that cause them, we can better understand how to deal with them. How do we do this? The diagram below shares the process that we'll explore in this section.

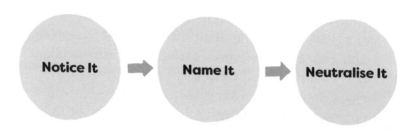

You'll find this technique, designed to help you transform your limiting beliefs, in many traditional cognitive-behavioural therapy (CBT) methods.[4] 'Notice it, Name it, Neutralise it' is a process that can be utilised in a variety of scenarios. It could be used to help you deal with limiting beliefs about an upcoming presentation, a cold calling blitz or the end of a quarter, ensuring that you focus on what you can control. It can also be used to reflect on past instances where limiting beliefs may have started to show up, such as a customer's reaction on a call, an email you receive from a colleague, or a lack of response from a prospect. In these situations, using this process can help you avoid overthinking or reacting irrationally.

How does it work?

Step 1: Notice It

The first step involves you becoming more aware of the event that's causing your limiting beliefs. Is it something coming up, like a performance review, or a situation that has already happened? Or, perhaps it's one that seems to be happening on an ongoing basis, like waiting for replies to proposals, prospects' reactions on the phone or feedback from your manager.

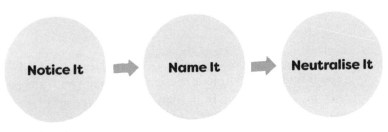

Step 1:
Notice the event
that is causing
the limiting belief

The point here is to start to identify a pattern. Is there a common situation or time when this is happening? The more you recognise this, the more you can be on the lookout for limiting beliefs and preempt them.

Inspirational Insights

Ellie Twigger, an Account Manager in the SaaS space, has first-hand experience with this. I met Ellie a few years back, and she's the kind of person you instantly warm to. Her personality and self-awareness are two of the many reasons she's now so well regarded by those around her in the SaaS world.

At the start of her sales career, Ellie was failing to connect with customers, and was losing deals and missing targets. But an important realisation helped her turn her fortunes around.

"I think being familiar with internal triggers is key here," she told me. "When I became present with how I was feeling, I could prevent myself from spiralling out of control, and stay in a healthy and positive mindset."

By recognising the events that triggered her limiting beliefs, she could catch them quickly, before they built up and became harder to manage.

However, it's also important to be mindful of how you notice these limiting beliefs. It can be very easy to be overly judgemental when they show up and we notice them. For example, you might find yourself ruminating over things like:

- 'Why am I thinking like this again?'
- 'I thought I'd managed to stop feeling anxious about this.'
- 'This is so frustrating.'

These kinds of responses can often amplify those thoughts and feelings, which may set off our primal brain response — doubt, insecurity, anxiety. Instead, try to stay neutral in how you respond to what you're noticing. For example:

- 'I'm starting to feel uncertain about this event again.'
- 'Here's that thought coming up again.'
- I'm noticing that I'm starting to overthink this situation.'

Doing this helps ensure that you stay in a rational head-space and are able to utilise the following step, which will be essential in transforming these thoughts and creating positive outcomes.

My Stories — The Dreaded Email

Early in my sales career, my trigger event used to be when an email came in from a particular manager. It would set off a set of limiting beliefs, sending me into a spiral of thinking that I'd done something wrong in my job and they were annoyed with me.

The negative outcome was me feeling anxious all day, until I eventually had a chance to speak to that manager in person. Sometimes I'd lose sleep if I didn't have an opportunity to do so until the following day.

I wasn't consciously aware of my trigger event and the irrational beliefs created by it, which led to negative outcomes. I eventually discovered this tool — 'Notice It' — and was able to utilise it to reconfigure these limiting beliefs and become more mindful of the event that sparked them.

Step 2: Name It

The next step is to identify and name the arising beliefs about the situation. What are all the things on your mind that are causing you to overthink upcoming events, or one that has occurred already? Responses that came up when I conducted a LinkedIn survey on this issue were things like:

- 'The demo won't go well.'
- 'I won't come across as senior enough for the people on the call.'
- 'They haven't replied because I've done something wrong.'
- 'That short email reply means I'm in trouble.'

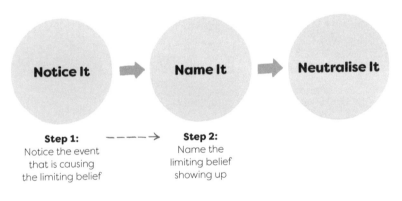

Step 1:
Notice the event
that is causing
the limiting belief

Step 2:
Name the
limiting belief
showing up

There are some really important benefits that can be gained from naming your limiting beliefs in a particular situation. First, you can take a step back and look at the self-talk statements that are holding you back or weighing you down. This gives you a focus, and is the starting point for gaining clarity on what you want to work on.

When going through this process, you must use the rational part of your brain, which interrupts your primal side. This means you can start to apply logic to these limiting beliefs, rather than letting them create irrational stories, convictions and phobias.

Noticing and naming your limiting beliefs is valuable, but it doesn't completely stop negative outcomes from occurring. This is where the third step, 'Neutralise It,' comes in. In the next chapter, we'll go through this measure and share two approaches you can take to effectively neutralise your limiting beliefs.

Your Three Key Takeaways:

1) When noticing your limiting beliefs, stay neutral in how you initially respond to them.

2) Naming your limiting beliefs can be an instant way to activate the rational part of your brain.

3) Acknowledging the negative outcomes generated by your limiting beliefs can create more purpose in wanting to tackle them.

CHAPTER 3

Neutralise Your Limiting Beliefs – Validate or Explore Them

Once you've identified events that are sparking your limiting beliefs and have named them, you then want to neutralise them.

To do this, I recommend two different approaches: validating them and/or exploring them. This allows us to avoid jumping to conclusions (such as why a prospect didn't reply) or always thinking the worst about an upcoming situation (like a sales pitch or demo). Instead, we focus on the facts surrounding a situation and neutralise limiting beliefs.

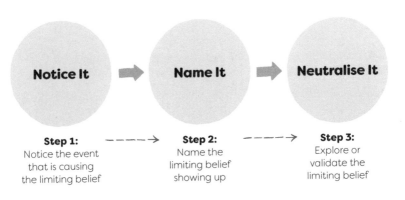

Notice It	**Name It**	**Neutralise It**

Step 1:	Step 2:	Step 3:
Notice the event that is causing the limiting belief	Name the limiting belief showing up	Explore or validate the limiting belief

Step 3: Neutralise It

Here's an overview of the two approaches you can take to neutralise your limiting beliefs, and when you might want to use them:

1. **Validate Your Thoughts:** If the limiting beliefs you've written down have happened already, or if it's a current situation, this step will help you explore any evidence behind the limiting beliefs and what else could be true in this situation.

2. **Explore Your Thoughts:** If the limiting beliefs you've noted down are based on an upcoming event, or if you've contrived a 'what if' statement, this step will help you pinpoint where those limiting beliefs are coming from, and what within your control can reduce the chances of it happening or prevent it entirely.

Below are some examples of when you might validate or explore your limiting beliefs. It may also be valuable in some cases to use both question pathways, to validate and explore them. This may be useful when limiting beliefs about a certain event are showing up in past, present and future situations.

Limiting Belief	Validate and/or Explore
A call you had yesterday that you're overthinking, convinced it went badly.	Validate
You have yet to receive a response from an email you sent to a prospect.	Validate
An upcoming one-on-one with a manager that you are dreading.	Explore
A big presentation scheduled for next week.	Explore
Doubting your ability as a manager.	Validate & Explore
It's one month away from end-of-quarter and you don't think you'll hit your target.	Validate & Explore

Activity A2 —
Validate or Explore Beliefs

Take some of your limiting beliefs (from Activity A1) and identify whether you are effectively validating (past event), exploring (future event) or both (past, present and future situations). Jot down your thoughts below.

Limiting Belief	Validate and/or Explore

Validating Your Beliefs to Break Free from the Sales Courtroom

Imagine that your mind is like a courtroom when it comes to limiting beliefs. There's 'the prosecution,' the primal brain, which focuses on the worst-case scenario and believes that everything has gone wrong with a past situation. This irrational prosecutor will throw out a variety of statements that, when combined with confirmation bias, we'll start believing are true.

Step 1: Establish the Facts

To avoid this, we want to validate our thought by creating a 'defence' to challenge the prosecution. The first question we want to ask ourselves with this mindset is:

1) Where is the evidence that this thought is true or false?

This step allows you to recognise that there often isn't any real evidence associated with this belief, meaning we can recognise that it's irrational. Our thoughts can appear very real until we ask this question and recognise them as just that, thoughts.

A follow-up question – 'How often is this happening?' – can be helpful if you do feel there's some form of evidence there. This question gives you context. For example, you may have had a particularly tough sales pitch a while back, but since then you've had 10-15 that have gone well.

Step 2: Acknowledge Other Possible Narratives

Once you've established that this is a limiting belief, and there isn't really any evidence to back it up, ask yourself this question:

2) What else could be true in this situation?

This allows you to explore alternative narratives and consider different possibilities. By asking this question we allow our brain to consider three or four different narratives, which means we avoid homing in on just one and creating a limiting belief around it.

Step 3: Reflect On How You'd Feel About Them

Now that you have these other possibilities, you want to ask yourself:

3) If I knew this other thought were true, how would I think or act differently in this situation?

Asking this can give you alternatives to how you would or could approach the situation. It again helps you to avoid feeling like you only have one choice or outcome, and means you can shift your perspective. Asking this question can even alter your emotions and feelings towards the situation, perhaps disarming yourself or self-soothing.

Last year, I was asked to create and conduct a training programme for a group of SDRs who were selling a computer hardware product. Managers in the team had noticed, after a couple months of consistently poor performance, that there were some common themes around limiting beliefs showing up in one-on-ones and performance reviews. A large percentage of the team were taking these at face value, and combined with confirmation bias, were creating bigger roadblocks to their success.

In the workshop, we focused on how to identify these limiting beliefs and take the steps outlined above, to validate them effectively. Overleaf are a couple of examples:

Limiting belief	Where is the evidence that this thought is true or false?	How often is this happening?
That prospect was short with me on a cold call because I did something wrong and am not good at speaking with C-level executives.	There isn't any real evidence to say I'm consistently bad at speaking with C-level people. It has happened 2-3 times in the last month, though.	I've made around 900 calls in the past month. This has only happened 2-3 times, which is around 0.3%.
My manager sent me a short Slack message about arranging an unexpected meeting. I must be in trouble.	There isn't any evidence. I'm making good progress in my role. There was one time I'd done something wrong, and the meeting made me feel stressed.	It's happened once in the 12 months I've been here. In that time, I've had 60+ meetings. So, that's around 1.5%.

What else could be true in this situation?	If I knew this other thought were true, how would I think or act differently in this situation?
They were having a stressful day and you caught them right in the middle of it. They would've behaved that way with anyone calling them at that time. It happens very little to me, which means I'm doing a good job, taking the right approach and can't control prospects' reactions like that.	I would avoid taking it personally. I'd feel a certain level of empathy towards them, rather than frustration.
They sent me a short message, as they're tied up in back-to-back meetings. They always send short messages like this; it doesn't mean I'm in trouble. This meeting could be positive, and/or the feedback will be useful to my professional development.	I wouldn't worry about this meeting all that much, as I know this is their style.

Bear in mind that not every thought you have is a limiting belief. If there is very real evidence and it's consistent, then it's not one. This exercise isn't about trying to prove that every thought we have isn't true; it's about spotting the irrational ones.

Activity A3 —
Validating Your Limiting Beliefs

For this activity, let's take some of the limiting beliefs that you noted down (based on past events) and validate them with these steps.

Limiting belief	Where is the evidence that this thought is true or false?	How often is this happening?	What else could be true in this situation?	If I knew this other thought were true, how would I think or act differently in this situation?

If you find these types of limiting beliefs showing up regularly, proactively schedule some time at the start and/ or end of your week to go through this. The more times you can practice and go through it, the more you're training your brain to think differently.

By asking these questions, you can begin to recognise and discredit your limiting beliefs based on a lack of evidence. You also start training your brain to avoid jumping to conclusions and consider what else could be true in a given situation.

The final piece of this, which is one of the most important steps, is to revisit this exercise once the situation has become clearer or played out to conclusion. For example, have a look back after you've delivered that presentation, had that meeting with your manager or received that email response. Often, we can feel relief when a negative situation or outcome, which we were convinced by some limiting thought would end badly, didn't turn out that way. This reflection is crucial as you further cement the reality of the situation, rather than locking in the limiting beliefs or irrational thoughts around it.

Let's say you thought a presentation you delivered went poorly, but then you receive feedback from your manager and the customer saying how pleased they were with it. Instead of just feeling relief, and moving on, revisit this exercise and go through what you thought was true and what turned out to actually be true.

The more you do this, the more you can remind yourself of the reality of these situations next time you're faced with a similar one. And then, when you get up to present, you can recall the feedback from last time and numerous other times, rather than the projected thoughts that have little or no evidence behind them.

Psyche Success Stories — Ryan & the Fateful One-on-One

I was working with Ryan, an experienced AE in a tech company, who'd convinced himself that every time he got an email scheduling a one-on-one with his manager, it was going to be about something he'd done wrong. As a result, he felt super anxious in the days leading up to the meeting, didn't focus on his job, made fewer calls and lost sleep.

Working with him on the question structure to validate his thoughts, Ryan was able to avoid jumping to that conclusion and recognise the value of the one-on-ones. He recalled that they were very rarely a negative experience, and when they were, it was actually constructive, as the feedback helped him improve in his role.

Ryan now looks forward to these sessions, and avoids jumping to conclusions when he gets an email from his manager.

Exploring Your Beliefs to Conquer the Negative 'What If' Sales Scenarios

When it comes to upcoming events, our limiting beliefs can start creating projections of what we think might happen, including imagining what could go wrong. Have you ever found yourself pondering countless 'what ifs' before a situation, filling you with stress and anxiety? They may sound something like this:

- What if this demo doesn't go well?
- What if I never achieve my target again?
- What if they judge me for what I say on this call?

Typically, it doesn't end there. We tend to craft an entire narrative around these dire thoughts. If that happens, it might sound like, 'What if I lose my job?' or 'What if that person lodges a complaint?' This cascading sequence of imagined events continues fuelling our apprehension.

These negative 'what ifs' are linked to our limiting beliefs and based on future events. They're stories we create in our minds, often before the first page of the book has even been written. The more time and energy we invest in them, the more tangible they seem, and the more stressed, anxious or overwhelmed we become.

However, we can learn to harness this conjecture. The objective is not to suppress it, but to explore and transform our thoughts and obstacles into actions that propel us forward in a proactive, preventive manner. Here's how:

Step 1: Identify the primary reasons behind the 'what if' thought.
Remember, the goal is not to prevent these thoughts from arising, but to alter our response to them. So, when these 'what ifs' arise, begin by asking yourself:
1) What are two or three key reasons why I believe this might happen?

   This inquiry prompts us to uncover potential blind spots in the given situation. These could be areas that we don't feel as knowledgeable about or prepared for, which is often what causes that anxious feeling. Asking this question allows you to dig under the surface of the emotion to find the root cause. Be sure to focus on actionable steps within your control, as opposed to uncontrollable circumstances like economic conditions or customer illness.

This initial step surfaces and lays all these reasons on the table, rather than keeping them confined to the realm of worry in our minds.

Step 2: Taking action. What can I do to avoid/ mitigate this potential outcome?

This stage involves taking those reasons that contribute to the 'what if' scenario and determining a tangible action within your control that can prevent or minimise the likelihood of it occurring. The objective here is to provide your mind with something actionable and future-oriented to focus on, instead of endlessly replaying a story that has not yet unfolded and may never happen. And then, the next question you can ask yourself is:

2) What are one or two things in my control that I can do to prevent or reduce the likelihood of this happening?

Over the past 12 months, I've worked with some 250 salespeople in individual one-on-one sessions, and this is one of the most common concerns I see holding them back from building a healthy and high-performing mind.

Opposite are examples of the prevalent negative 'what ifs' I've heard, the reasons behind them, and some practical and effective actions I've coached people through to prevent or reduce the likelihood of them happening.

Negative 'what if' (limiting belief based on the future).	Reasons why I believe this might happen.	One or two things in my control I can do to reduce the chances of this happening.
This demo won't go well	They ask me a question I don't know how to properly answer, or pose an objection. There is a prospect attending the demo who I don't know much about.	I can prepare for those questions ahead of time. Preempt that objection before they raise it. Research that person on LinkedIn beforehand. Ask my existing customer contact what is important to this other person.
This deal will not close in time for end-of-quarter	I haven't properly identified the urgency of the deal. I've only been speaking with one contact, not a wider group of stakeholders.	Identify the level of urgency in a follow-up call. Explore the impact of them not moving forward before end-of-quarter. Proactively reach out to them with valuable insights or a summary of the conversation so far.
I won't get this promotion	In the interview, I don't effectively answer the questions. I'm not displaying the necessary skills and behaviours, such as public speaking and leading team meetings.	See if you can get the questions ahead of the interview. Practise answering those questions and 'selling yourself' with someone already in that position. Lean into these activities, starting in small team settings and building on your skills.

As you can see, by going through these questions you can progress from a narrative that only fuels fear and anxiety to generating actionable steps that can now address solving or reducing the chances of these things happening.

Doing this creates a greater sense of control and certainty in a situation. The more we sit on the initial feeling, the more powerless we feel. By going through these questions, you translate a feeling into action.

Psyche Success Stories – Alice & the Upcoming Sales Pitch

I worked with Alice, an Account Manager, who would always dread an upcoming sales pitch. She'd feel stressed as soon as it was scheduled, and anxious about it for weeks, leading to overthinking the chances of it going wrong. She'd feel relief as soon as it was finished, only to have the cycle repeat itself with the next one.

The 'what if' we identified was Alice forgetting her proof points and/or not being able to answer specific questions. Once we identified this, we worked on actions she could take to preempt it. She began doing a run-through of the pitch with a colleague or manager in advance, where they'd throw out tough questions.

This made Alice more prepared and comfortable going into the pitch. It gave her tangible actions to focus on, which meant she wasn't overthinking the situation or building up more anxiety around it.

She has now made a habit of doing a run-through before every pitch, and no longer dreads the lead-up to these presentations.

Activity A4 —
Exploring Your Limiting Beliefs

For this exercise, let's take some of the future-focused limiting beliefs you noted down and explore them through a series of steps, using the grid below.

1. Take two of your forward-looking limiting beliefs — negative 'what ifs' related to something that hasn't happened yet — and write them down in column one.
2. For each, think about one or two reasons why you believe this might happen. Jot them down in the second column.
3. Now, ask yourself what two things in your control you can do to reduce the chances of or prevent this from happening. Note those down in the third column.

Negative 'what if' (limiting belief based on the future).	Reasons why I believe this might happen.	One or two things in my control I can do to reduce the chances of this happening.

By following this third step of neutralising your limiting beliefs, you can become more mindful of when they show up and avoid having them create negative outcomes. As in the previous chapter, reflection is also crucial here. In this case, it can be helpful to envision what would have happened if you hadn't taken those actions. For example, imagine that you hadn't preempted that objection, prepared for those questions or researched that person before the demo you were anxious about. How badly could things have gone if you hadn't proactively worked to make them go well?

Spending some time reflecting reinforces the benefit of these thoughts and how they're supporting you. Doing this over time will help you begin to build healthy new habits of thinking, which will further build your confidence and rational thought processes around how you approach these situations.

Your Three Key Takeaways:

1) Build a defensive posture in your mind: check where the evidence is, and what else proved to be true in previous situations.

2) Look under the surface of that 'what if' to understand why you think it may occur.

3) Focus on identifying proactive steps you can take to avoid limiting beliefs about future events that can cause things to spiral out of control.

CHAPTER 4

Mastering Your Mind – How Self-Talk Shapes Sales Success

How are you talking to yourself?

In sales, we often discuss how we can better communicate with our prospects and existing customers. We invest time in perfecting pitches for our products, companies and visions. However, we rarely prioritise the most crucial conversation of all: the one we have with ourselves.

The dialogue we engage in with ourselves, the 'self-talk' we've mentioned repeatedly here, sets the tone for every external conversation we have. We're often conscious of how others speak to us – whether they're colleagues, managers, prospects or friends – and will voice our disapproval when needed. But how often do we examine our self-talk? Very rarely.

Self-talk significantly impacts our state of mind and the narrative we construct for ourselves. Consequently, it influences our actions. This can help explain why you might question putting the same effort into making calls and reaching out on LinkedIn as you did last quarter, but are not achieving the same results.

Our minds are busy places. On average, we can speak about 130 words per minute (wpm). We can type 70-80 wpm, and in the song Rap God by Eminem, one of the fastest sections reaches 230 wpm.

Do you know what rate our self-talk operates at? Studies estimate it to be between 800-1,200 wpm. That's astonishing, right? If we aren't consciously influencing or challenging that conversation, it can run wild.

Consider your self-talk, here and now. Is it supportive and constructive, or overly judgemental and critical? Is it encouraging and motivating, or making you feel put upon and overwhelmed? Reflect on what you've said to yourself today. If it's critical, would you accept it if someone else, like your manager or friend, said it to you? If not, then don't accept it from yourself.

One immediate change you can make is to avoid using 'should/have to/need to' language.

Self-demanding words and phrases like these create pressure and judgement. Our primal brain dislikes being commanded. That's why we often engage in self-sabotage and procrastinate on tasks, only to berate ourselves afterwards for not completing them.

A simple reframing to try is using 'want to' or 'get to' instead. You *want to* do something, and you *get to* do so when you're ready, willing and able. This implies a sense of choice and puts you in control of the situation, as opposed to feeling like you're being dictated to. In particular, the phrase 'get to' can cultivate a feeling of gratitude, for having the personal freedom and latitude to consider doing something. You're telling yourself that you are in charge of your life.

I used to regularly find myself in this predicament, particularly in my late twenties, when I was selling sales training and had just moved to London. My usual unhelpful self-talk statements included:

- I should be going to the gym every day
- I need to eat more healthily
- I should read more about the industry I'm selling into
- I have to prospect every day

These statements were only hindering me, creating more judgement that I was underachieving and sometimes even self-sabotaging. I had the attitude, 'I'm an adult, I'll do what I want,' which was my primal brain jumping in.

When I started to become more conscious of this, I began to reframe these statements when they popped up with more supportive self-talk.

Unhelpful or judgemental self-talk	Supportive self-talk
I should be going to the gym every day.	I want to exercise 2-4 times this week, as it helps me reduce my stress.
I need to eat more healthily.	I want to eat a good balanced diet, during the work week at least, as it will make me feel good.
I should read more about the industry I'm selling into.	I get to have time in my day to learn more about the industry I'm selling into, which will help me better my performance.
I have to make cold calls every day.	I want to make cold calls each day to build my pipeline and make sure I'm consistent.

A simple reframing like this meant I was no longer feeling undue pressure or judgement from this self-talk. Instead, I found myself in control of it, and mindful of what it was going to do for me, by acting on it.

Inspirational Insights

"I can achieve more than the standard."

This is what Dale Dupree, founder of coaching and training company The Sales Rebellion, kept his self-talk focused on throughout his career. I met Dale through LinkedIn after reading numerous posts of his that, like this book, address topics not always covered in the world of sales. We sing from the same hymn sheet, so including him in this guide was a no-brainer.

Dale's story is a testament to the power of self-talk in overcoming adversity and achieving success. Battling childhood depression and surviving a suicide attempt, he grappled with debilitating self-doubt and limiting beliefs. However, through conscious efforts to reshape his inner dialogue, he began telling himself he could achieve more than the standard, the average, the norm.

This self-talk script supported Dale's new approach to how he sold. He set out to offer a completely different experience that was filled with authenticity and a human touch, not a stale, process-driven approach.

The impact was profound. Dale's win rates went from 30% to 80%, cold call conversions multiplied and sales cycles shortened significantly, from 6-8 months to 4 weeks. It was all fuelled by a newfound belief, driven by positive, supportive self-talk, in his ability to transcend the norm.

His journey underscores the pivotal role of self-talk in shaping outcomes, serving as an inspiring reminder that by mastering our inner dialogue, we can defy limitations and chart a course to extraordinary achievement.

"Nobody can make you believe," Dale told me. "But without it you'll build a silo where only you and your negative limiting beliefs exist, which no one else can get you out of."

Activity A5 —
Reframing Your Self-Talk

For this activity, consider some of those unhelpful or judgemental self-talk statements that may be showing up in your professional role or day-to-day life.

1. What are you feeling you 'should/have to/need to' be doing more of right now?
2. If that statement is coming primarily from your own self-talk and self-imposed pressure, jot it down in the first column below.
3. Now, how could you reframe that into more of a supportive self-talk statement ('want to/get to')?

Unhelpful or judgemental self-talk	Supportive self-talk

Action to embed the habit: If this is something that's showing up regularly, put a Post-it note reminder somewhere, drawing attention to this demanding self-talk. Or, tell a close friend or partner that you want to work on it. Ask them to flag it every time they hear a 'should/have to/ need to' statement from you, and remind you to flip over to 'want to/get to' instead.

Your Three Key Takeaways:

1) In assessing our self-talk, ask whether you'd accept a friend or colleague talking to you like that. If not, don't accept it from yourself.

2) Your self-talk is the most important conversation you can have. It will set the tone for how you approach and view each day, including challenging situations that may arise.

3) Be mindful of the demanding 'should/have to/need to' statements that pop up, and look to reframe them as 'want to/get to' opportunities.

CHAPTER 5

Moving Beyond Luck — Mastering the Controllables in Sales

It's not just the conversation we have with ourselves that's important, it's also the way we label and look at occurrences and events. A prime example is our perception and labelling of 'luck.' This word itself can be one of the biggest reasons we dwell on events and create strong, self-perpetuating limiting beliefs.

I was invited into a well-known sales engagement company, to work with their SDRs and AEs on reframing their self-talk. A key challenge the group was grappling with was that many of them were putting their success down to luck. They were also overly focused on being unlucky when they didn't close a deal or hit their targets. Superstition was rife in the organization — people seemed convinced that it was a roll of a dice either way for each deal. Here are some of the things they'd find themselves saying:

- 'I was so lucky to close that deal.'
- 'That person on my team always seems to have good luck when it comes to getting leads.'

- 'I always seem to have bad luck when it comes to my prospects postponing calls until next quarter.'

Luck is a common topic of conversation in sales. It can range from feeling lucky when we close a deal on the last day of the quarter, or feeling unlucky when one we were certain would be signed off by a prospect is put on hold due to a last-minute spending freeze. Unfortunately, constantly attributing success or failure to luck negatively affects your self-awareness, self-belief, confidence and performance.

First, let's say you close a deal or schedule a meeting, and you attribute it to luck. By doing so, you devalue the effort you put into it and deprive yourself of taking credit. Second, attributing success to luck prevents you from reflecting on what you did that made a difference. By attributing it to your lucky stars, you overlook the controllables: things you did well, actions that could be repeated for future wins.

Moreover, it leads to a sense of being less in control of every situation, believing that whether things go your way or not is determined by mythical luck. This mindset hinders recognition of your strengths, and what you're learning and improving upon along the way.

Conversely, if you believe you were unlucky, it can lead to a victim mentality, where you feel a sense of injustice and helplessness.

This, in turn, creates more frustration and drains your energy. Having this mindset will lead to a self-perpetuating cycle of instances where you feel wronged or that things just aren't fair. So, what's the solution? Instead of focusing on luck, concentrate on the controllables and uncontrollables.

Here are some examples of things that could be deemed controllable or uncontrollable in a sales situation:

Controllable	Uncontrollable
How many calls you make or emails you send per day.	The economy or market conditions.
Asking the right questions.	The prospect's business freezing expenditures.
Your mindset when approaching a demo.	When they started proactively looking for a solution.
How you plan and structure your day.	Your colleague picking up a lead when you're off.
What you do to reset yourself after a prospect is short with you.	Prospects taking holidays over the summer.
How you explain next steps.	Their previous experience with a similar product.

Now, look at ways of shifting your focus from perceiving things as lucky or unlucky to what you controlled and couldn't control.

Lucky/Unlucky perspective	Controllable/Uncontrollable perspective
I got lucky by winning a deal because I called when they were just about to start looking.	I engaged in meaningful conversations, asked the right questions, and identified the urgency and pain behind their needs. It also helped that I contacted them just as they began experiencing challenges in their business.
I was so unlucky not to close that deal. Why does this always happen to me?	It was frustrating not to close that deal, but I understand that I couldn't control the fact that they'd implemented a spending freeze. Next time, I could improve my research and qualification of the account, and get introduced to a few more people within the company. That could have helped me anticipate this situation sooner.

Isn't this approach more constructive and insightful? It means you're more mindful of what to focus on next time, it builds self-belief and it acknowledges your strengths, all of which increase your confidence.

Luck takes the power out of your hands and can reinforce limiting beliefs.

Focusing on the controllables directs your time and energy to where they matter. This prevents you from getting caught up in a sense of being treated unfairly and seeking justice. That's not to say these things shouldn't hurt;

they will. But it's not about stopping that feeling; it's knowing how to respond to it.

Another factor to consider with the uncontrollables is Egocentric Thinking, which was extensively studied by developmental psychologist Jean Piaget.[5] This is where you have a set of values and behaviours that you live by, and (consciously or subconsciously) expect everyone else to be the same.

For example, you may be someone who's not late for anything, never rude to anyone, or would never ignore a message. When you're on the receiving end of these behaviours, whether by a prospect, manager or friend, you instantly feel a sense of frustration, thinking they don't value or respect you.

We don't always need to accept the situation, decisions that have been made or the reasons, but instead accept we that can't control them. We can waste so much time and energy fretting over things that are simply out of our hands, feeling wronged, stressed and anxious.

Recognising what we can't control allows us to focus on the things that we can. Accepting that you can't control how sales targets are sometimes set allows you to concentrate on working out ways to reach them. Recognising that you can't control how a rude prospect spoke to you means you can channel your energy into finding others in the company who do want to talk with you.

The sooner you accept that a wall is a wall, the less effort you'll expend on trying to push it over.

Inspirational Insights

Sean Hayes, Global Business Development Director at Aircall, a cloud-based telecom service provider, is a big believer in this. I met Sean a few years back at a networking event. I've since been working with Aircall's go-to-market team in one-on-one coaching sessions. Sean and I have become good friends, and as he's an enthusiastic foodie, we've shared some good meals. It was at one such get-to-gether that we first delved into the 'luck' myth. Here are his thoughts on the matter:

"Even when salespeople hit their target, they can often feel like they got 'lucky.' I remember feeling this myself when I was younger, and I still feel it now at times.

"When salespeople say they feel lucky, I try to help them join the dots of their successes. I ask them to list their achievements or completed goals each week in one-to-ones, along with the 'one percents' — extra-mile efforts that nobody sees. These one percents are often things salespeople do naturally, like sending out 20 personalised videos or creating a new dashboard to better track activities. Making salespeople aware of one percents means they become more aware of these efforts and the impact they're having on their results. Over time, the one-to-one lists work as a logbook for successes and achievements, and point away from everything coming down to luck.

"When you realise that outcomes or achievements come from the effort you put in, you feel you can achieve anything. Hard work is humbling, as you see the results of your effort over time, but sometimes it still isn't enough to get the outcome or results you wanted. If you're conscious of the effort you put in, then the outcome affects you a lot less, good or bad.

This focus on the process, and being mindful of your efforts, can change the way you approach success and failure. If you don't let outcomes define you, you unshackle yourself from the fear of failure and you can do your very best work."

Activity A6 —
Defining Your Controllables

For this activity, consider a particular deal or the overall target you're thinking about consistently, and break down what's within your control.

1. Pick a specific deal/meeting/situation/overall target you're thinking a lot about.
2. Using the table below, write down the topic at hand and each thing or thought you believe you can control, or can't control, related to this.

Scenario:	
Controllable	**Uncontrollable**

Action to embed the habit: You might want to write this list out on a separate piece of paper, and have it somewhere you can easily refer to when you start pondering the overall situation again.

Doing this will help you avoid dwelling on what you can't control, and instead dedicate your time and energy to the things you can influence.

Your Three Key Takeaways:

1) Focusing on luck will lead you to ignore the things you did well to achieve an outcome, and make you more reliant on hoping uncontrollable factors go your way.

2) Luck will get you focusing too much externally, and on what other people are doing, rather than on what's within your control.

3) Identify and focus on the controllables. There are so many variables in our daily lives and our work in sales. Identify and focus your time and energy on what you can control. The sooner you accept that a wall is a wall, the less effort you'll expend on trying to push it over.

CHAPTER 6

From Comfort Zones to Familiar Zones – How Language Can Change Our Experiences

Take a moment to cross your arms across your chest, as you'd usually do so. Feels pretty normal, right? Now, cross them the other way, with the other arm on top. How does that feel?

You might say it's not normal, and sort of awkward. It may feel like that because it's something you've never really tried before. It's not necessarily uncomfortable, as much as it's *unfamiliar*.

We've spoken a lot about self-talk and the words we use that can hinder us, without us even realising it. In the world of sales, no day is the same, and we're continually having to learn and adapt. We may have to deal with a new product feature, a change in territory, our target market, and so on. All of this requires us to embrace change, which means regularly stepping outside our comfort zone. But what if I told you that one of the biggest limitations we could create for ourselves was continuing to label this as our comfort zone.

Instead, here are three reasons why it's more effective to start seeing it as your 'familiar zone.'

1. **Overcoming the perception of discomfort:** Calling our current situation a comfort zone implies that anything outside of it is uncomfortable. This perception can create unnecessary fear and resistance to stepping out of familiar territory and trying new things. There can even be a visible physical reaction – a grimace, or shaking our head from side to side – towards the thought of this new thing when we tell ourselves it's outside our comfort zone.

   By relabelling this as your familiar zone, we shift our perspective. We can start to recognise that what we perceive as the discomfort when trying something new is instead simply an unfamiliar feeling.

   This shift in perception allows us to approach new opportunities with an open mind, and reduces the bias towards perceiving them as uncomfortable. This could be applied to how you view cold calling, public speaking or learning a new hobby.

2. **Increased openness to new experiences:** Relabelling our comfort zone as the familiar zone helps us let go of preconceived notions about the discomfort of the unknown. We become more open to and less apprehensive about trying new things, embracing change and stepping outside of what we're familiar with. It broadens our horizons, exposing us to a wider range of experiences, leading to personal growth and development. As we embrace the unfamiliar and push our boundaries, our confidence grows, and we become more adaptable to different situations.

3. **Recognising the discomfort within the comfort zone:** While the term 'comfort zone' implies a place of ease and safety, the reality is that it can also be uncomfortable. Staying in our well-worn rut can lead to stagnation, boredom and a lack of fulfilment. Redefining it as the

familiar zone allows us to acknowledge the discomfort that can arise from staying in a familiar place and not taking risks. This recognition becomes a motivation to explore uncharted territory and seek new challenges, knowing that growth and personal development lie beyond the confines of our familiar zone.

When embarking on new endeavours, reframing the question from 'What if this doesn't work out and I fail?' to 'What's the impact if I don't attempt this and remain where I am?' further reinforces the importance of pushing beyond our familiar boundaries and taking action towards personal growth and success.

This gets your brain thinking about all the risks associated with staying in the same spot, versus just zeroing in on potential risks that come with making the change.

Situation	What's the impact of taking no action?
Starting to post on LinkedIn	• I miss out on potentially generating opportunities through the platform. • My personal brand becomes limited to just the company I'm currently with. • It becomes an even bigger fear hanging over my head.
Sharing more in team meetings	• My good ideas, which could end up helping others, don't get heard. • I don't build my internal brand. • I may get overlooked for future management positions that require public speaking.
Going for a promotion	• I stay in a job I may start to feel I've outgrown. • I don't get the interview experience. • I become annoyed with myself for not at least trying.

My Stories —
Reframing My Comfort Zone

About five years into my sales career, face-to-face pitches to numerous stakeholders became a requirement. Initially I saw this as outside my comfort zone, which led me to thinking the experience would be uncomfortable. This got me feeling anxious about the upcoming pitch, convinced it wouldn't be a good experience. This often had me wanting to just get through the ordeal, and focus on finishing it.

When I started to reframe this as my familiar zone, I began to see those feelings about pitching as unfamiliar, and not necessarily a bad thing. I reassured myself that the more I did it, the more familiar it would become. Not only did this reduce my anxiety leading up to the pitch, it encouraged me to embrace it as a chance to learn. I wasn't so focused on rushing to get through it, but rather on enjoying it and then reflecting on the experience.

As I got into the swing of this, I recognised that if I didn't expose myself to more sales pitches or recognise their value in my development, I wouldn't close deals and, as a result, I would lose out on future opportunities. Those included potential promotion to management roles where personal interaction, public speaking, storytelling and persuasive skills would be required.

Activity A7 —
Defining the Impact of Inaction

Take a moment to go through some of the situations that have been on your mind recently, where you feel you're avoiding or reluctant to try something because it doesn't feel familiar.

Write them down below, in the left column, and then note down some of the impacts that can come from taking no action.

Situation	What's the impact of taking no action?

Your Three Key Takeaways:

1) Labelling it as your comfort zone can lead you to instantly think everything outside of it will be uncomfortable, signalling your primal brain to procrastinate or avoid it entirely.

2) Reframing it as our familiar zone means we're more likely to step beyond it and avoid having it limit our potential and growth.

3) Rather than focusing on what might go wrong, ask yourself what's the impact of taking no action here.

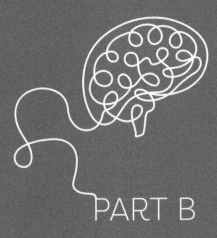

PART B

Harnessing the Emotional Rollercoaster of Sales

Being in sales is often referred to as an emotional roller-coaster. Within a day you can go through an array of feelings, from unbelievable highs when closing a deal to the lows that come from prospects and deals being postponed.

Your emotions, and how you understand, respond react to them, play a pivotal role in not just how you feel, but also your professional success. For example, a study by the management consultancy TalentSmart found that sales-people with high 'emotional intelligence' sell an average of $29,000 more per year[6] than those with lower levels. TalentSmart tested for this alongside 33 other important workplace skills and attributes, and found it to be the strongest predictor of performance, playing a direct role and contributing to 58% of success.[7]

In this second part of the guide, I'll take you through the importance of developing your emotional literacy, and how we can often mislabel or misunderstand our emotions. We'll examine how you can reframe your emotions as signals, rather than threats, and implement tools to improve how you respond, rather than react, to difficult situations. The final part of this will focus on that feeling of being overwhelmed, why it can occur and how to manage it.

This will help you build a healthier relationship with your emotions, and ratchet down the accompanying levels of stress. In doing so, you can channel your emotions into serving, not sabotaging, your mindset and sales success.

CHAPTER 7

Understanding Why Emotional Literacy Can Make or Break Your Sales Success

In sales, feelings of stress, performance anxiety or being completely overwhelmed can hijack your day, throwing the best-laid plans off track. This triggers a spiral of emotions that leave you feeling like a human punchbag, badly pummelled, down for the count and struggling to get back up.

Instead, to effectively acknowledge, identify and reframe your emotions, it's important to develop your emotional literacy.

Linked to emotional intelligence, emotional literacy is the ability to recognise, understand, manage and effectively communicate your own emotions, as well as those of others. It's key to how you respond in everyday situations, from handling a lengthening to-do list, a difficult call, a lost deal and everything in between.

This concept has been extensively discussed by the psychologist and science journalist Daniel Goleman, who popularized the concept in his book, *Emotional Intelligence: Why It Can Matter More Than IQ.*[8] The notion was originally put forth by the academic Peter Salovey and psychologist John D. Mayer.[9]

In this chapter we'll explore ways to build your emotional intelligence, first by sharing some of the challenges we can face from misunderstanding our emotions, and how to better acknowledge them, in order to build a healthy and high-performing approach.

Let's get into it with why our own vocabulary can be a roadblock to developing emotional literacy.

As with our thoughts and beliefs, the way we label and communicate our emotions can have a big influence on how we respond to them. In 2020, management consultancy Deloitte published a report, *Managing Emotions*, as part of its series on Empowered Wellbeing.[10]

This fascinating report included research from psychologist Robert Pluchik, whose work identifies more than 34,000 distinguishable human emotions, but notes that just 25 of them been named and appear in our vocabulary. You can imagine the confusion and difficulties this can cause in your professional and personal lives. Let's delve into some of those problems.

1. Mislabelling

How often do we find ourselves in situations where a lot is happening at once, and we automatically assume we're stressed? Perhaps you're behind on making quota, playing catch-up with your to-do list, or coming out of a particularly hectic quarter.

This assumption can often put our bodies into instant fight, flight, freeze or fawn states, making us even more stressed and anxious. Yet, behind that perception of stress could lie a range of other feelings.

Perhaps you're simply tired from a busy quarter, hungry after skipping lunch, unprepared for your day ahead.

Similarly, when it comes to anxiety, we might automatically attribute the sensations leading up to a call or presentation as anxiety.

However, it could also be excitement, nervousness, or feeling not entirely ready for what lies ahead. This mislabelling of emotions and jumping to a knee-jerk assumption can cause unnecessary stress for our bodies to deal with.

Psyche Success Stories — Marley & the Signal of Anticipation

Marley, an Enterprise Account Manager, had interpreted the feeling he got before a presentation as anxiety. He saw this sensation as a negative and would dread it, causing him to focus on all the things that would go wrong and ignoring his experience with countless other presentations that had gone well.

After I started working with Marley, he began to recognise that this labelling of anxiety before a presentation was actually anticipation, and a signal to pay attention to how he came across. Once he started reflecting on past presentations, he realised this feeling was actually helping him, getting him into a proactive, ready-for-action headspace.

After realising this and relabelling that feeling, Marley began to embrace it and effectively utilise it before presentations. He also spent time reflecting on the experience after presentations, recognising that those negative 'what ifs' rarely came to pass.

This process of cementing the reality of the situation helped him avoid negatively ruminating in the future.

And it's not just mislabelling of emotions that we can struggle with. Equally problematic is how we can sometimes label ourselves as the emotion.

2. Defining Yourself by The Emotion

In Part A, we touched upon the importance of self-talk and its powerful influence over us. It's crucial that we're also aware of how we express our emotions and the impact that can have. Here are some examples of statements you may find yourself making, related to how you're feeling.

> 'I'm so stressed,' after a busy week
> 'I'm really anxious about this,' in the lead-up to a big demo
> 'I'm not motivated,' on a sleepy Monday morning

Such statements can be an immediate trigger for your body's fight, flight, freeze or fawn response. This language implies complete immersion in that feeling, often fostering a sense of resignation that this is how you'll feel for the rest of the day, or the week. It can even cloud your view of your role itself, which leads to your emotions sabotaging your success. It's also a dead-end statement, offering no real solution to the feeling.

3. Assuming the opposite

Have you ever woken up and thought, 'I don't feel motivated,' and instantly concluded that you'll be demotivated for the whole day? Or, during a challenging week in your personal life, have you believed that you're an altogether unhappy person simply because you're not feeling particularly upbeat at the moment? You're not alone. We're too quick to assume that if we're not at the extreme end of an emotion, we must be at the opposite end of it.

In reality, there are countless shades of emotions in between the extremes that we might be experiencing. Hastily assuming the opposite and passing judgement on ourselves can be a self-fulfilling prophecy, bringing unnecessary stress and anxiety that get in the way of our activity. This can cause us to go into a day or week already feeling defeated.

Our statement	Our assumption
I don't feel motivated this week.	I must be an unmotivated person.
I'm not feeling particularly happy today.	That must mean I'm generally unhappy.
I don't feel completely confident about this call.	I'm not confident that this call, or any of them that lie ahead, will go well.

Developing your emotional literacy will enable you to be more mindful of these pitfalls. It can help you explore the true essence of your emotions, avoiding premature assumptions or labels.

The first step to doing this is acknowledging our emotions, rather than trying to fight or push them away. And then, we need to develop a better understanding of what their real purpose is, which is to be a signal, not a threat.

Your Three Key Takeaways:

1) Accurately labelling emotions prevents unnecessary stress and enhances performance, as illustrated by Marley's story.

2) Self-defining statements like 'I'm really stressed out' can reinforce negative feelings and hinder success. Reframe them with actionable solutions.

3) Avoiding assumptions about emotions' opposites fosters mindfulness, preventing self-fulfilling prophecies and enhancing emotional understanding.

CHAPTER 8

Emotions Are Signals, Not Threats

Imagine two of your friends at a theme park, sitting side by side on a rollercoaster. One hates the ride, while the other absolutely loves it. As they go around the track, plunging downward and rocketing into tight turns, they experience the same physical sensations: increased heart rate, disorientation, surging adrenaline and breathlessness.

However, their perception of these sensations will differ greatly. The one who hates rollercoasters will interpret the experience negatively, while the other will see it as a positive thrill.

Or, let's take another example specific to sales. One salesperson may see stress as a great feeling, helping them become more proactive and switched on with their calls or pitches. Meanwhile, another may feel overwhelmed by stress, causing them to not feel present when on calls. The sensation of stress will be the same for both, but their perception of it is dramatically different.

The point here is that emotions themselves are neither negative nor positive. There are only such things as positive or negative perceptions or reactions to an emotion. Likewise, stress in and of itself is not inherently negative or positive.

While stress may cause you to snap at a colleague or procrastinate, it can also push you to rise to the occasion and make you more proactive with your outreach.

The tendency to classify emotions as either positive or negative creates a problem. Emotions with negative labels become something we fear, leading to an even stronger negative reaction when we experience them.

This is where the Nocebo Effect can show up again. For example, if you believe the feelings you get when presenting are negative, you may be more likely to interpret normal physical sensations (like a fast heartbeat or sweating) as signs of stress or severe anxiety. This misinterpretation can exacerbate your emotional response, making you feel even more anxious. You may then develop a fear of presenting due to this interpretation of feelings.

On the other side of the coin, emotions with positive labels can drive us to constantly seek that feeling, perhaps by relying on strict deadlines or the sprint to the finish on the last day of the quarter. Excessive reliance on this can result in burnout and inaction when there's no pressure, such as at the beginning of a quarter.

Ultimately, all emotions serve as signals, not threats. Imagine them as a smoke alarm going off in your house. It's not necessarily indicating a raging fire, but it is something that requires your attention. We often treat emotions as if the house is on fire, triggering panic mode in our bodies.

For instance, when we start feeling anxious about a call or our quarterly performance, we begin creating stories in our minds about everything that could go wrong, tricking our primal brain into reactive mode.

It's equivalent to someone storming into your office and shouting, 'There's a fire! We're all trapped!' at the first sign of a funny smell. Instead, the emotion as a signal may be the equivalent of coming in and saying, 'Can somebody please check their food in the microwave? I think it's been on too long.'

By reframing our emotions as signals instead of threats, we avoid triggering our body into ultra-defence mode. Recognising emotions as signals is the first step to building a more effective and rational response to them, and ensuring that you're utilising them and allowing them to serve, not sabotage, you.

In addition to signals trying to get you to pay attention to something, emotions can also provide immense benefits in various situations.

Often, when we start to feel what we perceive as stress or anxiety, we label it very quickly and it can build up, feeling heavier and leaving us feeling more helpless.

The reason this happens is that sitting on an emotion can make us feel powerless. It seems uncontrollable. But if we can move through it, to identify an action at the end, we can start to take action.

This is again where the power of reframing statements into questions comes in, as discussed earlier. Going through the following mental exercise – a sort of internal Q&A – can prove quite helpful.

1. What do I believe I'm feeling?

You start by addressing the emotion you may often assume is showing up. For example, I'm feeling worried about this presentation.

2. What other emotion/feeling could this be?

This question prevents you from making a quick assumption and explores other possibilities. For instance, perhaps this is a sense of anticipation or excitement.

Yes, you might be anxious, but that's OK. These questions aren't trying to disprove your feelings.

3. **What is this emotion making me more aware of?**
This question gets you to start thinking about what the feeling might be trying to tell you, rather than how it's blocking you. It may be a signal to prepare for tough questions you don't know how to answer, or to go over the structure and flow of a presentation beforehand.

4. **What is the benefit of feeling like this?**
This begins to shift your mindset, helping you recognise not just the signal, but the value of the feeling. The more you recognise how your feelings are benefiting you, the more grateful and welcoming of them you can become over time. In this case, a feeling may benefit you by prompting better preparation for tough questions, because of the run-through beforehand.

It all comes down to context and understanding what your emotions are there for. Take the ringing of an alarm, for example. If it's a burglar alarm in your house, you panic because you suspect someone has broken in. But if it's a digital alarm on your laptop, reminding you to send an email, you appreciate it. Once you understand the context behind your emotion and the signal, versus the automatic perception of a threat, you can change how you respond to it.

There will of course be times where emotions *do* signal threats, but it's important to go through this question structure to validate before assuming.

Here's another angle on the previous four questions:

1. What do I believe I'm feeling?	2. What other emotion/ feeling could this be?	3. What is this emotion making me more aware of?	4. What is the benefit of feeling like this?
Anxious about an upcoming presentation	Anticipation Concern over lack of preparation Excitement	Prepare for questions Go over structure and flow of presentation	You go into the demo prepared and ready for what may be asked
Stressed about your target	Focused Heightened awareness Uncertainty	Stay consistent/ increase your outreach Focus on building a healthy pipeline Ensure that your forecasting is accurate	You focus on what's in your control and are proactive in achieving your target

Without these emotions/feelings showing up, the corresponding actions may not happen. The more you can recognise the benefits that come from them, the more you can build a healthier way to respond to your emotions and a level of gratitude towards them.

Psyche Success Stories — Archie & The Benefit of Stress

Meet Archie, an SDR who was constantly feeling stressed about his target of booking a certain number of meetings each month. I met Archie in a confidential one-on-one coaching session that his company, a cybersecurity firm, had contracted me for.

Archie initially saw this stress as a horrible feeling and wished he wasn't experiencing it, to the point where he'd started to question whether he was cut out for sales.

Among the exercises we worked through, we spent time identifying and creating a list of benefits that came from that stress.

The upside was that the stress made Archie more proactive with his daily outreach, stricter about his follow-ups, and not complacent after a particularly good week. All this showed that he cared a great deal about his performance, and the stress seemed to serve as a motivating kicker.

After recognising these benefits and regularly reminding himself of them, Archie's relationship with stress began to change. It was still there, but now that he saw the advantages, he perceived it as fuel — a positive thing.

Archie's main takeaway was that by changing his perspective on stress, he could utilise it far more effectively.

Activity B1 —
Recognising Your Signals & Benefits

Think about some of the emotions that show up regularly in your role, and go through those same four questions to become more aware of the potential signals and benefits they provide. Jot down your observations below.

1. What do I believe I'm feeling?	2. What other emotion/ feeling could this be?	3. What is this emotion making me more aware of?	4. What is the benefit of feeling like this?

Remember to avoid self-judgement and stay neutral when your emotions show up, as mentioned in the 'Notice It' section.

Your Three Key Takeaways:

1) Developing your emotional literacy involves understanding the nuances of emotions beyond basic labels, avoiding mislabelling, self-identification and assumptions about opposite emotions.

2) Emotions are signals, not threats. Ask what they're trying to tell you and how you can respond to them.

3) Recognising the benefits of an emotion or feeling can ensure that you build a healthier relationship with it, and know how you utilise it when it shows up.

CHAPTER 9

Mastering Your Self-Regulation

A big factor in how we initially acknowledge and respond rationally to our emotions comes from how quickly we can activate our rational brain to do so. If we don't, that emotional response will often be irrational, driven by the primal brain, leading to situations that we look back on with regret.

Think about a situation where someone triggers you. It could be a difficult prospect, an email postponing a deal or an unexpected 'no.' In response, we tend to react negatively.

We might snap back at someone or impulsively send a note we later regret. Our thoughts may instantly turn negative – we won't reach our targets; our day/week/quarter is ruined; maybe we're not cut out for this after all.

Often, this boils down to a lack of self-regulation, allowing our emotions to overpower us. We can come to believe that every emotion is a commandment we must act on, there and then, rather than a signal, as discussed above.

Self-regulation refers to the ability to monitor, control and manage your thoughts, emotions and behaviours in order to achieve your goals, adapt to changing circumstances and maintain a healthy mind.

In sales, as in life, we can't control many external events, but we can always control how we choose to respond. Below we'll look at a tool to help with that, and it only takes 90 seconds.

The 90-Second Window

As neuroanatomist Dr. Jill Bolte Taylor explains in her book, *My Stroke of Insight*, "When a person has a reaction to something in their environment, there's a 90-second chemical process that occurs; any lingering emotional response is simply the person choosing to remain in that emotional loop."[11]

Scientists have found that constantly reacting to things beyond our control not only leads to unhappiness, it sets off a stressful biochemical cycle that weakens the immune system. As such, chronic reactivity literally shortens our lives.

When those unexpected events occur, our bodies activate a physiological dump of chemicals into our system to help deal with it, thinking we're under threat. It's a bit like bouncers storming into a club because they think they heard a glass smash or shouting.

When our bodies are in this state, they are ready to fight, flight, freeze or fawn. And if we react without thinking, we justify that feeling sticking around for longer. A bit like knocking a glass over or continuing to shout when the bouncers come in — they're not leaving.

Enter the 90-second window, a practical tool to practise and utilise in situations where you encounter unexpected news or events. Per Taylor's book, studies have shown that within 90 seconds of a surprise occurrence, our minds and bodies can reset themselves back to their default state. It's often our reaction, rather than the situation itself, that keeps us in that irrational state for longer.

This tool will enhance your effectiveness in managing such situations and increase your ability to respond intentionally, rather than reacting irrationally. And so, when those bouncers come bowling in, they soon recognise that there's no issue and leave.

Note that it's important to use these types of tools before you need them. If all you do is turn to them in heat-of-the-moment emergencies, you start to regard them in a negative light.

It's why some people see the gym, or certain foods, negatively – they only use them when they're in a reactive state and feel like they 'have to' get fit or eat more healthily.

Here are the steps to implementing the 90-second window:

1. Pull a stopwatch up on your smartwatch or phone (after switching to aeroplane mode to avoid any distractions) and click start.

2. Focus on counting, in your head or out loud, up to 90 seconds.

3. While doing this, focus on your breathing – four seconds in, four seconds hold, four seconds out, four seconds hold. This is called Box Breathing .

If you can change up your environment for this, it helps. Get away from your desk to a sofa, or outside the office.

If you've just tried this out, what did you notice? Probably a sense of calm and clarity.

There are three things happening here:

1. **Counting to 90 seconds stops your primal brain from taking over.**
   When counting, you have to use the rational part of your brain. Remember, you can't use both parts at once. This stops the primal brain from jumping in with a story, self-criticism or a reaction that you later regret.

2. **You observe your emotions versus reacting to them.**
   When doing this, you can start to notice what's happening in your body: where the blood flow is going, how the body cools itself down, etc.

   This can be an empowering experience as you start to recognise and reinforce that emotions are signals, not mandates that we must follow instantly, and they can disappear as quickly as they appear.

3. **You can decide how to respond instead of instantly reacting.**
   After the 90 seconds, you'll find yourself in a more rational headspace, allowing you to make a decision consciously, rather than just reacting reflexively.

The Five Senses Exercise

Being in sales often means your mind can feel like a busy, even frantic, place. That's particularly the case on those days where you're jumping from meeting to meeting or only taking five minutes for lunch. Another tool to utilise within the 90-second window that can help you deal with these days is linked to mindfulness.

Mindfulness is a powerful practice that promotes present-moment awareness. This can get a bad rap, mischaracterised as you needing to be in a dark, silent room, sitting with your thoughts for 30 minutes. While building up to this level can be useful, there are some smaller steps you can take to start incorporating mindfulness into your day.

One of them is the Five Senses Exercise, which we'll put into perspective here first, and then step through. This practice can be helpful on those days where calls and emails are starting to become a little overwhelming. It can help kickstart your day or end it, and make you feel more present with friends and family during your evenings and weekends.

The exercise is a grounding technique commonly used in mindfulness and cognitive behavioural therapy, to help manage anxiety and stress by focusing on your immediate sensory experiences.[12]

It encourages you to engage with your five senses – sight, touch, hearing, smell and taste – to bring your focus to the present moment and quiet all that noise going on.

Engaging in mindfulness activities like this on a regular basis can deliver a number of direct benefits not just for your mindset, but also your sales skills.

What can it help with?

1. **Stress Reduction:** Whenever you're feeling stressed, anxious or overwhelmed, perhaps from a difficult call or meeting, taking a few minutes to engage in the Five Senses Exercise can help calm your mind and reduce stress.

2. **Sharpen Focus:** You can use this exercise before meetings, pitches or interactions with prospects and customers to sharpen your focus and improve your ability to read cues and respond effectively.

3. **Better Communication:** By being present in the moment, you can communicate more effectively and avoid having your primal brain jump in with irrational thoughts and reactions.

4. **Decision-Making:** Enhanced concentration and emotional regulation can assist in making well-informed decisions during sales processes, such as how to re-engage a prospect who's gone quiet or work through tough negotiations.

Psyche Success Stories — Farah & The Five Senses

Farah, an Account Manager with a couple of years' experience, found that stress brought on by small moments — an unexpected email, a rearranged meeting schedule, a postponed deal— would completely derail her day, and potentially the entire week.

She'd lose focus and ruminate on this, which was not only affecting her performance, but also her ability to switch off outside of work. She often took the stressors home, which was straining her personal relationships.

As part of working with Farah, I introduced her to the Five Senses Exercise, to utilise along with some other tools. As a result, she started to gain more control over her reactions and adopt a more thoughtful problem-solving approach when things came up.

She found the exercise helped her reset, and it had a positive impact on her productivity, and various interactions during the work day and at home, as she wasn't carrying the stress.

Activity B2 —
The Five Senses Exercise

Step 1: Find a Space
Start by finding a quiet and comfortable place where you won't be disturbed. If that's not possible, this exercise can be done at your desk.

Step 2: Set a Time Limit
Decide how long you want to practise the exercise. It can be as short as a few minutes or as long as you feel comfortable extending it. I'd suggest that 2-5 minutes is a good starting point.

Step 3: Begin with Breathing
Close your eyes and take a few deep breaths to centre yourself. This helps in transitioning from the busyness of your day to a state of mindfulness.

Step 4: Go Through Your Five Senses
You won't need to write any of the following down; simply acknowledging it in your mind is effective in this case.

A) Five things you can see: Open your eyes and take in your surroundings, trying to notice things you don't always acknowledge (what's on the walls, how the ceiling looks, the corners of the room).

B) Four things you can hear: Now, if you feel comfortable, this is when you'd close your eyes. Shift your attention to your sense of hearing. Listen to the sounds around you (music, background conversation, something outside, the noise of an appliance).

C) Three things you can feel: Bring awareness to your sense of touch, and what you can feel with your hands or on your body (what your hands are resting on, clothes on your skin, the chair, the floor under your feet).

D) Two things you can taste: Next, focus on what you can taste in your mouth. If you have something nearby, take a sip or bite of it, opening your eyes for a moment to avoid any accidents. Otherwise, it could simply be the taste of fresh breath.

E) One thing you can smell: Finally, explore your sense of smell. Take a few deep breaths and notice any scents in the air or on your skin (aftershave, perfume, pets, flowers, a fresh breeze blowing in through the window).

After you've spent time with each sense, gradually bring your attention back to your breath. Take a few deep, calming breaths, and when you're ready, open your eyes. Reflect on how you feel at this moment.

The general response I get from salespeople I work with using this technique is a sense of calm. They report their mind feeling less busy and more present.

Another tip is to think of this as similar to drinking water – you don't just have one sip a day and that's it. Instead of saying, 'I did the Five Senses thing a couple of hours ago ... I wonder why I'm feeling stressed again,' see it as an ongoing exercise that can deliver benefits at a moment's notice. As such, put it into regular practice, giving your mind those moments to reset throughout the day.

Action to embed habit: Think of 2-3 times a day where you can start building the Five Senses Exercise into your routine. It could be when you wake up, on your commute to work, after leaving the office or before bed. This will help you become more familiar with it, and prepared to utilise it when needed.

Your Three Key Takeaways:

1) You might not always be able to control what happens, but you can work on your self-regulation to control how you reasonably respond to it, rather than impulsively react.

2) It takes 90 seconds for your mind to reset itself from a stressful state to a neutral one. See that you're giving it the space to do so.

3) Utilise the Five Senses Exercise to reset your mind throughout the day. The more you use it proactively, the less you'll need it reactively.

CHAPTER 10

Handling the Dreaded Feeling of Being Overwhelmed

In the fast-paced world of sales, the pressure to meet targets, close deals and exceed expectations can often feel overwhelming. But what exactly does it mean to be overwhelmed?

At its core, it's an intense feeling of an inability to cope with the demands placed upon us, either internally or externally. It's that sensation of drowning in a sea of tasks, deadlines, demands and expectations, unsure of where to turn or how to stay afloat.

When this feeling is building up, each missed opportunity or rejected proposal adds another layer of stress, leaving you feeling inundated and uncertain about what path to take.

You can associate the feeling of being overwhelmed with things such as a racing heartbeat, shallow breathing or tension in your muscles as your body reacts to the stress. Mentally, you may feel scatter-brained, unable to concentrate or make decisions effectively.

Emotionally, you might oscillate between feelings of frustration, anxiety and self-doubt, sometimes questioning whether you can get past this, or even whether this sales game is really for you.

At the height of being overwhelmed, you could find yourself struggling to maintain motivation and confidence in your abilities. What once seemed like exciting challenges may now feel like insurmountable obstacles, casting a shadow over your enthusiasm for the job and life in general.

Three Hidden Reasons Why Overwhelm Occurs

We've touched on some of the more obvious contributors to this sense of being hopelessly buried, like having an excessive workload coupled with limited timeframes. But here are some other factors to be aware of:

1. **Lack of Prioritisation:** When you're unsure about which tasks to prioritise, or how to effectively manage your time, it becomes difficult to handle everything simultaneously. Your primal brain, which can't tell the difference between the past, present and future, often looks at all of these unorganised priorities and feels they all have to be done at once. This can create a sense of overwhelming helplessness as you struggle with where to start and how to proceed.

2. **Perfectionism:** Striving for perfection or setting unrealistically high standards can be a major contributor to feeling overwhelmed. The fear of making mistakes or not meeting your own expectations can create constant pressure that becomes unbearable over time. You will find a lot of 'should/have to/need to' language here, often stemming from internal self-talk, and that only adds to the stress.

3. **Boundaries Not Being Set:** Difficulty saying no or failing to setting boundaries can lead to taking on more
than you can handle. This can result in a crushing accumulation of responsibilities and commitments. You try
to maintain a brave front, and look like you're in control, but under the surface you can really be struggling.
And now, there's the added fear of disappointing those
around you, who you've already said yes to, regarding
additional tasks and responsibilities.

Psyche Success Stories – Warren & The Controllables

Meet Warren, a newly promoted Sales Manager for a fintech
company. I started working with Warren after he came across
me on LinkedIn and signed up for one-on-one coaching.

Despite success in his career, the demands of this new role
left him constantly feeling behind and out of control. He
was fighting the battle of hiding this feeling from his team,
but it would show up through snappy responses or reactions to reasonable questions.

Together, we identified triggers and patterns contributing
to Warren's feeling of being snowed under. We focused on
the controllable aspects he could influence, his self-talk,
and more reflection on past experiences where he'd felt
buried and managed to rise above it

As Warren implemented these strategies, he began to
feel calmer about the new job and more in control of
things. Even on particularly hectic days, he was able to

self-regulate, and instead of impulsively reacting he was now responding with intention.

He then began to share these tools with his team, to help others deal with the daily stresses and proactively avoid becoming overwhelmed.

At this point, you're probably already thinking about the tools and techniques we've been covering, and how they can support you in managing feelings of being overwhelmed.

Here are some other useful ways to handle, and proactively prevent, these feelings:

Five Ways To Manage & Prevent Feeling Overwhelmed

1. Avoid 'should/shouldn't' statements

All emotions are natural and serve a purpose. When feeling overwhelmed, try to avoid telling yourself that you should or should not feel a certain way. As mentioned earlier, this only creates more pressure and judgement. Instead, focus on controllable aspects and identify one or two things you can do to feel more comfortable or confident in the situation. Ask the question, 'What are 2-3 things in my control right now that I can focus on to reduce/remove this feeling?'

2. Remember that it's often a breakdown of thoughts, not always of life

The sense of being overwhelmed often arises from an overload of thoughts. Remind yourself that nothing may have actually changed yet, but your thought process has. By staying present and reassuring yourself that nothing has happened, you can bring reassurance to your primal brain.

Telling yourself that you have time to prepare for 'it,' if and when it comes around, you'll ease into taking it step-by-step. Using the Explore Questions we discussed in Part A of Chapter 3, you can focus on preparing for the future change rather than fearing it.

3. Recall previous experiences

This probably isn't the first time in your life you've felt overwhelmed. The situation may differ, but the sensation and actual experience often hasn't. Reflect on past instances of feeling underwater, and how you managed them. Remind yourself of the tools and strategies you used, what you told yourself and how you got through it last time.

By doing this, you reassure yourself and build confidence. Having dealt with these past experiences, you're better equipped to deal with the current situation.

4. Communicate

Like many emotions and thoughts, it's easy to think you're the only one experiencing them and are therefore reluctant to talk about them.

The value of talking with others isn't always to find a quick fix or bulletproof solution, but to first make sense of your thoughts. Choose someone who will listen without immediately trying to offer those quick fixes or contributing to the sense of being overwhelmed.

Telling the person that you aren't looking for a solution, just a friendly ear, can be helpful, as it avoids them assuming they need to find an answer.

5. Write it Down

A big contributor to feeling overwhelmed is having all these thoughts spinning around in our head. Imagine being told you have to solve a jigsaw puzzle, but you can only look at all the pieces piled in the box. Impossible, right?

You'd want to throw them out on the table and start by finding the corner edges and joining things up. This is what happens when we write our thoughts down; we can look at them from a bigger and more logical perspective.

When you start to notice feelings of being overwhelmed, get a pen and paper and jot down what's coursing through your mind. Don't worry about getting it any particular order. Doing this will help you focus your time and energy on what's currently happening, and what you can control, versus projecting what might happen in the future.

Your Three Key Takeaways:

1) Being overwhelmed can often be a breakdown of thoughts, not life itself. It can occur when it feels like there's an influx of potential change, demands or challenges.

2) Be mindful of managing the hidden causes of burnout, which include a lack of prioritization, rigid perfectionism and boundary-setting issues.

3) Take action by avoiding judgemental statements, staying present, recalling past successes, communicating with others and writing down your thoughts, all of which will contribute to regaining control.

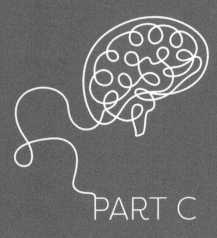

Unlocking the True Meanings of Motivation

You won't go a day in sales without hearing the word motivation. It's often seen or positioned as the essential fuel to your engine, necessary to propel you towards your sales goals. However, it's often misunderstood, and in this part of the book we'll address why and how to properly generate and utilise motivation.

First we'll cover why it's important to be conscious of your proverbial 'hospital' – a metaphor we'll use to represent the 'why' behind all your hard work – to spark motivation. Next, we'll look at understanding whether your motivation is intrinsic (personally satisfying) or extrinsic (driven by external rewards). We'll then ensure that you're pointing in the right direction with your motivation, and looking to move towards, and not solely away from, something.

Along the way, we'll bust some motivation myths, such as thinking you should be constantly motivated, and that motivation is always needed to take action. Plus, why having a 'surfer mentality' when it comes to motivation can serve you well in sales.

You'll finish this part of the guide with all the ingredients and tools needed to fully master your motivation, understand how to take control of generating it, whilst being less reliant on it, to build a consistent level of high performance.

CHAPTER 11

Building Your Hospital, Walls & Bricks

One day, a person walking past a building site became curious about what was being constructed. He asked a worker, "What are you doing?" The worker responded, "I'm laying bricks."

Dissatisfied with the answer, he asked the worker next to the first one, who said, "I'm building a wall." Feeling like they were part of a joke, the person went further along and asked a third worker, some distance from the first two, "What are you doing?" The worker responded, "Building a hospital."

All three were right with their answers, and each response was equally important. Without the bricks being laid, there is no wall. Without the walls being built, there is no hospital.

This analogy is an important one to think about when it comes to motivation, to make sure you know what you're building towards. That will help ensure that you're on the right path, and make clear what you can focus on each day, week and month to get there. Let's break each of these down in more detail.

Your Hospital

Your hospital – your 'why' that's steering you towards your ultimate objective – needs to be something you spend time exploring the reasoning behind and having a clear understanding of. Without it, those tough moments and setbacks may make you question why you're in the sales game.

It's also one of the biggest reasons I see salespeople struggling with motivation in the first place. They haven't defined their 'why,' and without something clear to work towards, there isn't any incentive to pick up the tools and start building. It's a bit like not having a destination to walk towards; there's really no reason to get up and start walking.

I also see salespeople who think they have their 'why' defined, but it's often a cursory, surface-level thing. For example, the most common ones are to make money, to get promoted, etc. But there's more work to do here.

For instance, why do you want to make money? What will you do with that money? Perhaps you want to make money to buy a house. Why do you want to do that? Is it because you grew up in a rented flat and owning a home would make you feel secure and proud of yourself? All of a sudden, this 'why' (hospital) of yours becomes deeper than just money. It has more meaning and resonance.

The clearer you become on why you're doing what you're doing, the more motivation you'll create to do so, and the more resilience you'll develop to overcome any challenges along the way.

It's also important to avoid just having one hospital to focus on. Make sure you've got a few mixed in, reflecting your work and personal life, to avoid placing your identity, time and energy in one basket and neglecting other areas of your life.

Explore your 'why' and the reasons behind it. This may change as you grow and progress through your career, which is natural, so don't hesitate to revisit it.

Your Hospital (your 'why')	Why do you want this?	And why is that?	And why is that important to you?
To make more money.	To buy a house.	My parents never owned their own home.	I want a place to call home, and the pride that comes with being able to do this.
To get promoted.	To make a bigger impact and support others.	I feel fulfilled when I see others being successful.	It drives my purpose and what makes me feel valued.
To run a marathon.	To challenge myself and test my limits.	I want to prove to myself that I can still learn and adapt to challenges.	I've let self-doubt sabotage situations before, but not this time.

Your Walls

Now for the walls of your hospital. These are mini-goals to get you there. Sometimes we set big goals that are exciting, but seem so far away, like wanting to climb a mountain but standing at the bottom and not knowing how one goes about scaling it.

Some days, looking at the snowy peak can seem daunting, and downright unachievable. Instead, setting your sights on the first base camp and aiming for that, feels more achievable. For example, when you go for a run, it's about focusing on little landmarks along the way, versus thinking about the entire long and winding route.

If your goal is to be promoted, for example, it calls for breaking down the milestones along the way. What are some of the skills you need to develop? What do you need to achieve by the end of the month or the quarter? What are some things you can start learning now that would be useful in the new role? Whose radar should you get on in senior management, who can help you along towards your career goals? Giving yourself these 'walls' provides short-term, realistically attainable goals to focus on.

Without the walls, building that hospital won't happen. Your 'why' will often feel too far away, and this causes people to procrastinate or give up on their goals entirely. Break them down into more easily constructed pieces to ensure that you don't give yourself distant milestones. This will also provide ways to recognise your progress along the way, which can help build momentum and increase motivation.

Your Bricks

You can have the most exciting goals, and mini-goals to get there, but without action they won't be attainable. That's a primary reason salespeople struggle with goal setting: they fail to adopt the habits and pursue the actions needed to achieve them. They get too wrapped up in where they want to be, projecting ahead to the outcome, neglecting the present reality and the process necessary to get them there.

Your bricks should be actions you take on a daily or weekly basis, that are in your control, to help you construct the walls and ultimately build your hospital.

For example, with a promotion in mind, perhaps your daily action would be making a certain number of calls and learning a few helpful new things a week about your industry, company or potential new role. It may also be looking for one or two opportunities a month to present in front of a group, or leading a session on new developments in your industry or an approach that's working for you.

Taking actions that are in your control ensures that you're constantly laying bricks, assembling walls and building your hospital, instead of just dreaming about it. The more actions you carry through on, the more in control you'll feel about the outcome.

Remember, if you get lost in daydreaming about your hospital, it won't get built.

If you get too focused on your bricks, you'll lose the meaning behind what you're building and might give up.

If you don't set your walls, your hospital will feel too far out of reach.

Treat all these elements with equal respect and thought.

With these three things in mind, let's see what they look like together.

What's your hospital? (Goal)	What are your walls? (Mini-Goals)	What are your bricks? (Habits)
Getting promoted to Team Lead	• Identify areas of strength and which aspects you want to work on. • Find an external mentor to learn from. • Seek opportunity to cover as team lead when manager is away.	• 1-2 hours a week of personal development. • Networking three times a month. • Maintaining a productive level of activity in your role each day.
Becoming comfortable with public speaking	• Be able to run a solo presentation within three months. • Deliver one speech at a local event within six months. • Join a public speaking club.	• Practice presenting in front of a mirror 1-2 times a week. • Read 3-5 pages of a book on these skills each day. • Observe 1-2 people a week presenting, in person or online.
Running a marathon	• Aim for under a certain time in a 5k run. • Complete a half marathon within six months. • After nine months, achieve a sustainable marathon-length pace.	• 13-20km of running per week (increasing over time). • Weekly mobility training. • One long run, sprint session and splits each week. • Track progress and times.

Inspirational Insights

Ursula Llabres, Director of Customer Growth at Meta's Reality Labs, has some valuable thoughts on the importance of defining your bricks. We met after Sales Psyche began supporting Meta, providing Ursula and other leaders with one-on-one coaching. I enjoy my conversations with Ursula and am inspired by her passion for continually testing her own limits. Here are her thoughts on this topic:

"When I encounter new situations, my initial response is to take a deep breath, pause to process, and then break down the challenge into smaller, manageable steps. As an ultramarathoner, I've learnt that even the most formidable runs can be conquered by simply taking that first step, then another, and another.

"Viewing the problem as a whole can often be overwhelming and lead to paralysis. Deconstructing it and reassembling the solution piece by piece is less intimidating and far more manageable. Even in moments when I failed, I have not given up, but taken the time to understand what happened and how I can learn from this."

As Ursula makes clear, the value of the bricks is not something to overlook. They are controllable, small steps to get you where you want to be.

Activity C1 — Defining Your Hospital, Walls & Bricks

Take some time now to think about two of your own goals (hospitals), in your career and outside of it. What are some walls you can use to signal that you're on the right track and help break down that goal? Finally, what are some daily or weekly habits you can focus on that will help get you there? Jot these down in the grid below.

What's your hospital? (Goal)	What are your walls? (Mini-Goals)	What are your bricks? (Habits)

Your Three Key Takeaways:

1) Your Hospital (Goal): Define your deep-rooted motivations, beyond surface-level goals, as they provide clarity and resilience in navigating challenges.

2) Your Walls (Mini-Goals): Break down long-term aspirations into manageable milestones, to help maintain focus, track progress and build momentum.

3) Your Bricks (Habits): Take consistent, intentional actions aligned with your goals to lay the foundation for success, ensuring progress towards your desired outcomes.

CHAPTER 12

Defining Your Sales Drive – Navigating Intrinsic & Extrinsic Motivation

Defining your hospital, walls and bricks is an important aspect of creating motivation, but it's also vital to understand what type of motivation is driving you to want to build your version of a hospital. Is it intrinsic or extrinsic?

Understanding intrinsic and extrinsic motivation is pivotal, due to their profound impact on your mindset, performance, job satisfaction and overall success. This has been extensively studied by psychologists Edward L. Deci and Richard M. Ryan.[13] Here are some examples of how your motivation for a task may differ, depending on whether it's intrinsic or extrinsic impetus that's driving you.

The task	Intrinsic motivation	Extrinsic motivation
Learning about a new product	Genuine curiosity about it, an opportunity to grow your knowledge base and a chance to think creatively about how you'd position it to prospects.	To gain recognition for mastering knowledge about the new product, and additional commission generated by deals to be had.
Learning a new approach to prospecting	Enjoying the process of learning, finding new ways to interact and challenging yourself to improve your skills.	Thinking it will make you look good to others, wanting colleagues to ask you about it, or because your manager asked you to learn more.
Building trust with customers	Genuine interest in understanding them, and as a result knowing you're helping them achieve their goals.	You may get referrals as a result of the trust you've built, and be able to upsell in the future with them.
Exercising	Doing it because you find it enjoyable, and it allows you to take care of your health and fitness.	To achieve a specific weight loss goal, or to win a fitness challenge with a reward.
Learning about your industry	You have a genuine interest in the topic, or find pleasure in expanding your knowledge and imagination.	To impress others, or because your manager has asked you to do so.

Extrinsic motivation – Driven by the outcome that will result from doing the task

Extrinsic motivation is likely the one you'll be most familiar with, characterised as behaviour that's driven by external rewards or incentives. These lures can be tangible, such as money, trophies, perks or promotions. Additionally, they can take on psychological forms, such as praise and public acclaim. Extrinsic motivation relies on external factors to drive and reinforce your behaviour and actions.

Extrinsic motivation plays an important role in various aspects of life and sales. It can provide you with tangible benefits and incentives that drive self-betterment, productivity and achievement.

For example, the promise of a bonus or commission serves as a big extrinsic motivator for you to hit or exceed targets and expectations. These external rewards can stimulate salespeople to put in additional time, work harder and stay focused on specific goals.

Moreover, extrinsic motivation can provide you with external validation and recognition. Praise and public acclaim for accomplishments can boost confidence, self-esteem, credibility, your personal brand and a sense of accomplishment.

However, it's worth noting that too much of a focus on extrinsic motivation can make you overly reliant on external validation and recognition. This dependence on external approval may lead to a diminished sense of self-awareness and self-confidence, as you become more concerned with meeting others' expectations and less aware of your own internal drive.

Additionally, an overemphasis on extrinsic motivators can hinder your ability to work towards goals that lack clear deadlines or tangible rewards, as you may struggle to find motivation without immediate external incentives. That's why it's so important to bear in mind your intrinsic motivators.

Intrinsic Motivation – Driven by interest in and enjoyment of the task itself

At the same time, why is this more inner-focused, self-generated sense of intrinsic motivation important? It immerses you in your tasks, sparking deep engagement, enhancing focus, creativity and performance.

Intrinsic motivation is driven by you and your own curiosity, self-determination and purpose. Tasks, goals and habits driven by intrinsic motivation will often be the ones you're the most consistent with and get the most enjoyment from. Furthermore, they're a potent catalyst for personal growth.

Pursuing your passions and values in and outside your sales career drives continuous learning, skill mastery and a growth mindset. This cycle of self-improvement bolsters competence and motivation, and – as with extrinsic motivation – it can influence your credibility and personal brand.

However, be wary of the Overjustification Effect, a concept extensively studied by psychologist Edward L. Deci.[14] This can occur when you introduce external rewards (extrinsic motivation) for intrinsically (personally) rewarding activities. This can serve to diminish that intrinsic spark.

For example, you may really enjoy walking, but being part of a walking challenge at work could diminish your enjoyment of it. Or, you may like video prospecting, but if it becomes a key performance indicator, your enjoyment of it may drop off.

It's great to have those constant extrinsic motivators in sales – commission, bonuses, President's Club and other incentives – but it's important to not be solely focused and reliant on them.

Becoming more mindful of your intrinsic motivation is an important part of building your bigger picture, and adding more depth and meaning to what you're doing. I'm not talking about having to completely love the product you sell, but rather knowing what selling it can enable you to do, learn and achieve.

Activity C2 — Identifying Your Intrinsic & Extrinsic Motivators

Take a few minutes to write down what you feel are some of your intrinsic and extrinsic motivations, not just in your professional role, but across all aspects of your day-to-day life. This could be linked to hobbies, a side hustle and so on.

Intrinsic Motivators	Extrinsic Motivators

Managers should always be looking to encourage and understand your intrinsic and extrinsic motivation, but they should never be responsible for your motivation.

You may have noticed that extrinsic motivation is driven by things, not other people. This is associated with a common myth I see among salespeople, who believe their manager or company are responsible for motivating them. That's just not true.

In the pages ahead we'll address three of the biggest myths associated with motivation. Let's start with one I just mentioned.

Motivation Myth #1: Managers and companies are responsible for motivating their teams

Sometimes, we mistakenly believe that it's someone else's duty to motivate us, whether it's our manager, senior team members or those around us. The reality is that no single person can motivate another.

They can inspire us, but they can't provide motivation. Believing that it's solely your manager's responsibility to motivate you can lead to an unhealthy reliance on them. You may think that if they're not present or they're not supporting you, you won't be successful. In that case, when your manager takes a holiday, or receives a promotion, or the team expands and you spend less quality time with them, you might start doubting your own performance.

When we think about motivation, we often overlook aspiration and inspiration. Aspiration is your hospital (your 'why'). Imagine inspiration like the blueprint plans of how you're going to build the hospital, along with images of other hospitals to give you an idea of what's possible.

For the managers reading this, placing excessive pressure on yourself, thinking you need to have all the answers to motivate your team, is counterproductive. Instead, it's about empowering and inspiring them to motivate themselves.

#1 Truth: A manager's responsibility is not to motivate you to build your hospital. Rather, it is to inspire, provide a blueprint, give salespeople an idea of what they can achieve and where they can go, and guide them on how to get there. To do this a manager should focus more on creating an environment that fosters motivation and provides inspiration.

Your Three Key Takeaways:

1) Extrinsic Motivation is driven by external rewards, which can boost productivity and confidence. But, be mindful of it leading to potential dependency on external validation.

2) Intrinsic Motivation stems from genuine interest, curiosity or enjoyment of the task itself, and is important for creativity and personal growth. Yet, it may diminish if external rewards are then attached to it.

3) While managers can inspire and provide guidance, true motivation comes from you, which will contribute to regaining control.

CHAPTER 13

Identifying the Direction of Your Goals

When thinking about what motivates you, it's also important to consider the direction of your goals. Are you trying to move away from or towards something?

Ensuring that your motivation is being driven in the right direction is important. Too often, I see salespeople and leaders fail to change a bad habit, overcome obstacles and reach their objectives because they're concentrating on 'away-focused' goals, rather than 'towards-focused' ones.

Here are some examples of how the two compare:

Away-focused goals	Towards-focused goals
I need to stop talking so much on discovery calls.	I want to ask at least 3-5 more questions during my discovery calls.
I want to stop spending so much time on my phone in the evening.	I want to start reading 3-5 pages a night.
I need to hit my target to avoid being put on a personal improvement plan.	I want to hit that target to support my progress and book that holiday I want for next year. To get there, here are the activities I'm going to focus on each day.
I need to stop feeling so anxious about this presentation.	I want to feel more prepared for this presentation by doing a run-through and preparing for 3-5 questions I think they're likely to ask.
I really should go for a walk to help me stop feeling so tense.	I want to go for a walk because it's a soothing activity I really enjoy.
I need to stop responding to my emails/Slack messages so frequently.	I want to break my day up into 8-10 segments to better focus on what I'm doing.
I need to stop sitting at my desk all day and getting stressed.	I want to exercise for 30 minutes a day and get out for a walk at lunchtime.

You can see key differences between towards-focused and away-focused goals, and probably recognise some statements you've been saying to yourself.

Away-focused goals are when your main driver for doing something is to escape from that feeling, avoid an activity, or stop doing a certain task. Towards-focused goals are when your main driver is to achieve a certain feeling, complete a task or create a specific habit.

Here are four areas that can be impacted by away- or towards-focused goals.

1. The Direction You're Going In

Imagine you arrive at a restaurant and are waiting to be seated. A waiter comes past and says, 'You can't stand there. Can you move please?' So you move, but he comes back and asks you to move again. You're likely to ask, 'Well, where can I stand then?"

Without direction, you can find yourself in all sorts of spots that still aren't right. This is the first problem with away-focused goals: they lack direction.

When you're trying to move away from something, how do you know that the direction you're heading in is the right one? You could tell 100 salespeople they need to stop talking so much on discovery calls, and you'd find that some would become too blunt, whilst some would ask fewer questions. And, some may change their behaviour for a bit, but go back to being overly talkative. The point is that it wouldn't be a helpful instruction.

The other challenge with not having a clear direction is that by moving away from something, you can find yourself encountering new challenges. For example, you may say you need to stop spending so much time on your phone in the evening, but you then end up spending more time watching TV, and not really achieving what you want.

Or, you may say you need to stop sounding so 'salesy' on cold calls, but you end up coming across as too relaxed and overly familiar with prospects.

Towards-focused goals give you this direction. If you told those same 100 salespeople a more effective way to handle discovery calls – sharing examples of what this looks like and how to tighten their opener and questions – you'd see a lot more consistent behaviour across the board.

When you know where you're going, you give yourself a clearer direction to work towards, meaning you spend your time and energy in the right places.

You also avoid jumping from one challenge to another. So, that example of wanting to spend less time on your phone in the evening becomes spending more time reading. You now give yourself something more productive to do with that time; something to work towards.

2. How You Measure Your Progress

Another challenge that comes from away-focused goals is that they're hard to measure. How do you know when you've actually stopped talking so much on discovery calls or stopped spending so much time on your phone?

How can you quantify 'less of' or 'so much,' which are inherently imprecise? You can't. And so, you won't recognise progress towards what you're focusing on, and you'll start to lose motivation and hope of achieving it.

Towards-focused goals solve this dilemma, as they make it far easier to measure and recognise your progress. If your towards-focused goal for discovery calls was to ask 2-3 more in-depth questions, you could easily recognise when you start doing this and feel good about the change you're making.

On that note, be sure that when you're defining your towards-focused goals, they are specific. For example, saying you want to get better at cold calling or improve your nutrition is too broad. Instead, you might say you want to improve cold calling by scheduling a one-hour block for calls each day, doing research in a separate 30-minute period beforehand, and speaking to one or two colleagues a week to learn what works for them. Likewise, tell yourself you're going to eat more nutritionally by having a plant-based dinner three nights a week and cutting out sweet, fizzy drinks entirely.

3. Your Consistency

Imagine you're standing on a street corner, waiting for a friend, and you catch a whiff of a bad smell. You move a few metres away, until you stop smelling it, but moments later it returns, and this pattern repeats itself.

The same can happen with away-focused goals. They can prompt action, but not long-term change, because once we feel we've escaped this feeling or thing we tend to stop.

It's why some people who set a goal of losing weight, and achieve it, go back to their old eating habits and put the pounds back on. Or why someone who's anxious about a presentation may get through it with some reactive coping mechanisms, but then find themself experiencing the same cycle of anxiety the next time they're asked to present.

Being solely motivated to move away from something won't often lead to sustainable change or consistency in the long run. On the other hand, the benefit of towards-focused goals is that they can create healthy habits and consistency that stretch beyond your initial focus.

For example, with presenting, your towards-focus may be that you want to feel more prepared by doing a run-through and rehearsing answers to 3-5 questions you think your customers are likely to ask.

This will not only give you tangible things to focus on to reduce your anxiety, but it helps establish good habits around planning for presentations. Towards-focus means you don't just look for something to paper over the cracks. You're proactive, and give yourself tools and more consistent ways of achieving something.

4. What You're Focusing On

Constantly reminding yourself of the thing you're trying to avoid or prevent is stressful. It's like someone constantly telling you 'Don't screw this one up' when you're about to present. It can lead to nerves, fumbling over words and stilted delivery.

Looking back to what we discussed about negative 'what ifs,' the other problem here is that because you're constantly thinking about what you want to avoid, you might start to make assumptions that it will happen, creating more stress and anxiety.

Towards-focused goals give you something more positive to think about and work towards. Visualising this adds to that motivation, as it gets you to start imagining what it will feel or look like once you achieve it. Projecting the future outcome can spark present feelings and thoughts that support you in getting there. It also makes it feel more like a choice that you have, rather than a demand upon you.

Note that away-focused goals aren't all bad, and shouldn't be avoided completely. Incorporating an element of these along with towards-focused goals can help you anticipate and navigate potential obstacles more effectively. It also instils a healthy awareness of the potential risks and pitfalls, and can spark proactive measures to mitigate them.

In situations where immediate threats or challenges arise, away-focused goals can also provide the necessary drive and urgency to address them quickly.

When you're focusing on something you want to do, always ask whether you're being driven towards a feeling or away from it.

Activity C3 —
Creating Your Towards-Focused Goals

Take some time now to reflect on what is currently motivating you in your role, or outside of work, and the goals associated with it. Write down how you might view this situation, and then some ways you can make these goals towards-focused.

Current focus	Towards-focused goals

Your Three Key Takeaways:

1) The impact of being solely driven by away-focused goals is that they often lack direction, are hard to measure progress on, and often lead to short-term actions without sustainable change.

2) Towards-focused goals give you more clarity, help you track and measure progress, and build sustainable change and habits in the long run.

3) While towards-focused goals are generally more effective for long-term change, incorporating elements of away-focused goals can help anticipate obstacles and address immediate challenges, striking a balance between proactive planning and urgent action.

CHAPTER 14

Adopting the Surfer Mentality for Motivation

There's an idea perpetuated by what we see online and how we perceive others around us – such as colleagues and top performers showcased on social media, and people who always seem to be living large – that constant motivation is possible. This is another of the big myths associated with motivation.

Motivation Myth #2: You should be constantly motivated

We assume these individuals are always motivated, upbeat, positive, focused and productive. In reality, motivation is not a bottomless well we can tap into on demand. It comes in peaks and valleys. It is unrealistic to expect ourselves to always stay motivated.

When we're motivated, we expend a significant amount of energy and focus. That's why we often feel exhausted after those high points, when we've been truly driven and excited by certain events, like a big deal we closed or the first few days after the end of a high-flying quarter.

The belief that we should constantly be motivated negatively impacts us because when we're not feeling particularly determined, we tend to self-judge, doubt our abilities and beat ourselves up. Thoughts like 'I felt so motivated last week' or 'I should feel motivated considering what I have the opportunity to earn' ironically make us feel demotivated and have a negative impact on our wellbeing.

The defeatist mindset we can default to is one where we feel like we'll always be where we are. When we're super psyched up, we sometimes perceive that that's how it will always be, and then wonder where it's gone and feel badly when that feeling subsides.

Conversely, when we're feeling low or floundering, we can struggle to see the light at the end of the tunnel and feel as though we'll always be stuck here. This is linked to affective forecasting: our ability, or lack thereof, to predict our emotional future. Our primal brain, which can only think in the present tense, can create those irrational stories we spoke about, where we feel like nothing is going to change. To avoid this, focus on building, what I call, a Surfer Mentality.

#2 Truth: Motivation isn't a destination we can reach, whereby we always feel motivated. It comes in waves, and these waves are something we can influence and become more aware of, as I'll now explain.

The Surfer Mentality

A healthier way to look at motivation is by imagining it as waves that undulate up and down. You can control certain elements of the wave, and what you do while on it or under it. To embrace this approach and avoid the belief that you should always feel motivated, look at adopting the Surfer Mentality.

It's easy to get caught up in different feelings in sales, from the exhilarating highs you get from closing a deal, to the lows of missing a target, or getting an email saying a customer needs to push a deal out to the next quarter. You can go from feeling like you've finally cracked it to wondering whether you'll ever book a demo or close a deal again.

It helps to imagine sales (and life) as a series of waves, rather than linear moments. Some days (or moments) you'll feel like you're riding the crest of a perfect wave, and other times you'll feel like you're under one, being helplessly tossed about. The key here is to acknowledge that wherever you are, you're not stuck there. There's always that next wave, which is on the horizon, building momentum.

The Surfer Mentality is knowing that no matter how good the wave you're riding is, eventually it will dissipate. If you spend time wondering where it's gone, or focusing on the uncontrollables, you'll find yourself flailing around underwater and miss the next one.

So, what can you do to craft the Surfer Mentality? Focus on what you can do when you're riding a wave, as well as when you're under one.

Riding the wave of motivation

This mentality is about being conscious of what you did to get on that wave in the first place, focusing on the controllables we discussed earlier.

In those months or quarters when you feel like you're an invincible closing machine, signing deal after deal and feeling super motivated, ensure that you make time to not just celebrate success, but analyse it.

It's easy to get caught up in the positive feelings – to bask in those shout-outs in the group chat or on the leaderboard and revel in the drinks that evening – but be sure you're making time to become more self-aware of what you were thinking and doing to get into that situation.

If you spend days overthinking why you missed a target, spend equal time reflecting when you do hit a target. Do so personally and as a team, analysing the successful quarters in the same way you would those more difficult ones.

The more mindful you become of this, the more you'll be able to replicate it or bring yourself back to it when that wave of motivation starts to drop. It's often easier and quicker to repeat something you're already doing than to change something you're not.

And again, when you do this, be conscious of zeroing in on the controllables in the situation and not just on external factors or luck.

Ask this helpful question when doing this self-assessment: 'What have I been thinking, feeling or doing to achieve this?'

For example, it could be:

- Supportive self-talk, focusing on what you can control in calls and presentations, not what could go wrong
- Feeling calmer and more centred, as you've been getting 6-8 hours of sleep a night and exercising 2-3 times a week

- Feeling more prepared by planning your week on the previous Friday, and sticking to set blocks of time for outreach each day
- Split-testing your calls – trying subtly different tactics with different subsets of prospects, and seeing which ones work better – to get an idea of new approaches to use
- Thinking more about your short-term goal of getting promoted to a Team Lead role
- Catching up with friends, either in-person or over the phone, a couple of times a week

Becoming more conscious of how you influenced your success will help build self-belief and confidence for the future.

Inspirational Insights

Abi Williams, CRO at strategic consulting firm Lead Not Lag, emphasises the importance of recognising what you're doing when riding a wave and the strengths you're displaying.

"It's key that we know what our strength is, nurture it and be proud of it," she told me. "In the past I had a leader try to tell me I needed to work on a competency that I and others know was already a strength of mine. This was due to the leader's own inferiority complex. If I had not intentionally worked on the awareness of my strength, I would have perhaps doubted myself or changed what I was doing.

"Self-development and self-awareness are paramount here. I took steps to identify my strengths and ask others where they thought my strengths lie. I then identified the gaps, alignment and intention, and worked on specific competencies to showcase my strengths. I also had a coach who helped me confidently articulate and develop my strengths.

"Identify where your strengths are and master them. Make them visible, for you to see and call upon."

Activity C4 —
Reflecting on Your Success

For this activity, I want you to think about a particularly good deal, month or quarter you've worked on recently. Ask yourself what you were you thinking , feeling or doing that made it successful.

What is the positive situation you want to reflect on (quarter, week or specific deal you closed)?

What were you thinking, feeling or doing to achieve this?

Dealing with being under a wave

When you're submerged under a wave and wondering where the motivation has gone, it's about first of all focusing on pushing yourself back to the surface. Too many times salespeople focus on getting back to feeling super motivated and riding their peak wave.

This can feel very far from reach, and can cause you to feel more demotivated as a result.

In the moments where you feel like you're under that wave, rather than judging yourself or wondering where the previous wave went, focus on what you can control.

When we're too focused on uncontrollables, we stay underwater longer. That can be accompanied by feeling a sense of injustice, that it just isn't fair. We can't control this; it's a reminder that life isn't meant to be fair.

The more you focus on what you can control when under a wave, the more you can pull yourself to the surface, rather than feeling even more submerged by all the things you can't control. The reason you write down and acknowledge what you can't control is to avoid wasting time and energy on it.

Psyche Success Stories —
Warren & the Controllables

A few years back, I was working with Rayan, an Account Manager. He'd been grappling with what he believed was his biggest problem: not feeling like he was constantly motivated.

He'd go through phases of feeling totally focused and aligned with what he was doing, buzzing to get to work. Then, there would be days or weeks of wondering where it went. This meant his numbers were inconsistent, and he'd begun feeling anxious and beating himself up over this unpredictability.

His biggest challenge wasn't the feeling of not being constantly motivated, it was his belief that he should be.

Once he became more mindful of the waves, and not expecting motivation to constantly be there, he found he was judging himself less in moments where he was under-motivated and focusing on what he could control.

He was also able to become more consistent with his performance as he became more aware of what he was thinking and doing.

Rayan has now advanced into a Team Lead role and regularly references the Surfer Mentality to his team.

Having this mindset outside the office, in one's in day-to-day life, is also a great way to handle the inevitable ups and downs. We can't expect anything to last forever. I'm not suggesting a pessimistic outlook, but a more realistic way of acknowledging and accepting the uncontrollables, and focusing on the controllables within.

Your Three Key Takeaways:

1) Motivation can come in waves. Recognise what is working when you're riding one, and how you can be consistent with those thoughts and actions.

2) Be conscious of focusing on what you can control when under a wave, to pull yourself out of it and avoid dwelling on the feeling that you're underwater.

3) Keep the Surfer Mentality in mind. Motivation won't always be at a consistent high point. Ride the waves and deal with the falls.

CHAPTER 15

Don't Wait for Motivation, Create It

If you're a runner, into hitting the gym, take morning walks or have any other hobby, you've probably had those days where you just don't feel like getting up and doing it. You're lying in bed, perfectly comfortable, and every part of you resists the idea.

However, you're still likely to go ahead and do it because it's a habit, or because you remind yourself of how you'll feel afterwards. So, you push yourself to go to the gym or take that walk. And how do you feel at the end? Motivated! It's the old adage that we never regret a workout.

This links to the third biggest myth about motivation, which is that it's required in order to take action. That's not true. Instead, by engaging in the action itself, you can generate motivation.

Motivation Myth #3: You need motivation to take action

The myth surrounding this notion is that we always need to feel like doing something in order to do it. With this belief, when we lack motivation, it either prevents us from taking action or we approach it with the sense that we won't be successful.

Whether it's a cold call blitz, LinkedIn research, exercise or any number of hobbies, the crucial point is that if we simply wait for motivation before acting, we waste time and energy. It's often the case that motivation is waiting for us to act before it kicks in.

This myth also stems from what we first think of when someone asks what motivates us.

When I ask most salespeople this question, I'll get the following answers:

- Money
- Progression
- Staying healthy
- Family
- Being financially secure

You may have noted some of these down a few pages earlier. There's nothing wrong with them, but do you notice a common theme? They're all outcome-focused, pointing to a destination to get to or maintain.

We've discussed the importance of having your hospital, and how if that's all you focus on, some days it'll seem so far out of reach, difficult to picture, and you'll struggle with your motivation.

This is where the value of your bricks comes in. It's not just because they're controllable, but they can give you more action-based motivators, rather than just out-come-oriented ones.

Having action-related motivators helps reinforce the notion that action can create motivation, and that we don't always need to rely on motivation to create action. For example, some actions that create motivation could be:

- Putting on a favourite music playlist
- Going for a walk to get some fresh air before working from home
- Reflecting on your hospital and walls (your 'why' and checkpoints)
- Doing a breathing exercise
- Watching a YouTube guitar lesson
- Looking back and reflecting on your progress so far

These motivators are actions you take that you know will get you into a positive headspace and make you feel good, whether for work or in your day-to-day life, for overall mental wellbeing.

Here are two questions to ask yourself to assist with focusing more on action-based motivation (bricks) than just your outcome-oriented ones (hospital).

1. **What can I do now to spark my motivation?**
   Imagine a car sitting on a driveway on a cold day. It may struggle to start, not because there's anything wrong with it, but because it needs to warm up. This is what we need on some days where we feel a little slow, and maybe not at our sharpest.

   Instead of simply saying 'I don't feel motivated to do ...' ask the question above. What can you do to jump-start your motivation? As discussed in the first part of the guide, this activates your rational brain. It gets you thinking of what's in your control that could spark the motivation required for a specific task, a big-picture activity, or life in general. Do not simply expect motivation to be there waiting for us.

Activity C5 — Defining Your Action- Related Motivators

Take a moment to write down some of the action-related motivators that you do, or could, utilise on a daily or weekly basis:

Answers

2. How will I feel after doing this task/activity?

Think about any habit you already have in your life. It could be that daily walk or workout at the gym, early morning journalling, or blending up a green smoothie.

When you think of any habit you already have, you often don't think about how you feel now, but instead focus on and remind yourself of how you'll feel after you've done it. It's that clear-headed feeling after a run, the sense of achievement after booking a meeting from cold calling, or the satisfaction that comes with sharing a nice home-cooked meal. This is future-focused thinking, stemming from habits you already have.

But this is often what's missing for those tasks and actions that aren't quite habitual, go-to bricks yet. With these we tend to focus too much on the process beforehand and how we feel in the moment, which stops us from taking action. Instead, ask yourself how you'll feel after doing this task or activity.

Here are some examples of this:

How I feel now	How will I feel after doing this activity or task?
I don't feel motivated for cold calling.	By making a few calls this morning I'll feel like I've warmed up, and built a bit of momentum for the week ahead.
I'm not feeling particularly pumped about the day ahead.	By spending an hour at the gym before work I'll feel energised and focused through the day.
I'm not really up to doing video outreach at the moment.	Once I've recorded one video, I'll feel in the zone and ready to do more.

A little tip that I suggest to a lot of people is voice-noting yourself after you've done an activity or task. Literally leave yourself a phone message reflecting how well something turned out, and give it a listen at a later date. It's a good thing to reflect back on and spark future motivation, just as holiday photos or videos bring back happy memories and make you want to book another trip.

#3 Truth: Action can spark motivation. Instead of waiting for motivation to come along, focus on actions in your control to spark motivation. Often, starting a task will generate that momentum and motivation from it.

My Stories –
The Motivation To Write

I want to share something I experienced, related to everything we've been talking about here regarding motivation. It's based on this very guide you're reading.

I'm going to be honest with you. Have I been consistently motivated to write this guide? No I haven't, but I've consistently utilised all the tools and techniques we've been covering here to support me in this process.

I identified my hospital, walls and bricks early on, with the main focus being producing this guide. The walls were the different chapters and sections along the way, which I gave myself weekly goals to work towards. The bricks, my habits, were allocating a certain amount of time for the work each day.

At the outset, I reflected on my intrinsic motivation for writing the guide, tying it back to my passion and personal experience of struggling with these aspects in my career. I wanted to provide a resource that would help salespeople and leaders understand that they're not alone in what they're thinking or feeling. And, that there are tools, techniques and practices that can help us identify and deal with those natural, all-too-common feelings.

I've also spent time reflecting on the weeks where I've been really productive with writing, and what I'd done or thought about during those times to achieve this. When I haven't felt motivated to start writing or proofreading my work, I've focused on actions to create motivation. That included everything from walking, exercising and listening to music, to imagining someone picking this up and reading it.

The process of writing has helped me reflect on what's really important to cover in this part of the guide. It's helped me trim the fat and focus on the key ingredients.

I've also learnt a lot about myself along the way, and it's elevated my awareness of my own motivators.

Your Three Key Takeaways:

1) Instead of waiting for motivation to strike, make the first move. Motivation won't always be there waiting for you; you have to create it.

2) When thinking about what motivates you, don't just focus on the outcomes (money, a promotion, etc.). Consider controllable actions (exercise, music, advice from colleagues).

3) Contemplate how you'll feel after completing a task, rather than before doing so, to spark motivation.

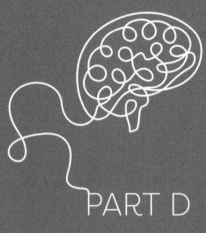

PART D

Learning From the Setbacks in Sales

Sales can be a rewarding yet tough, challenging career choice, and setbacks are an inevitable part of the job. From losing a big deal to dealing with rejection, setbacks can have a profound impact on our mindset and mental wellbeing. It's easy to get caught up in negative emotions, doubt yourself and sometimes even question whether the sales game is for you.

To avoid this, it's essential to develop resilience. You must learn how to deal with setbacks, like missing targets, deals being postponed, not getting a promotion or disruptive shifts in your market segment or the broader economy.

Having resilience allows you to bounce back from these disappointments, maintaining the momentum and enthusiasm necessary to push on through.

In this part of the guide we'll explore some common myths, and then break resilience down into five characteristics. This will give you a greater understanding of where your strengths already lie and what you can work on to develop your resilience.

You'll learn about three types of knockbacks you can face in sales, and why the word 'failure' is often misused. Finally, we'll focus on feedback, an essential part in continuing to learn, but one that cause you to become fearful and defensive. We'll talk about how to embrace feedback and how to be proactive with seeking it.

You'll leave this part of the guide knowing how to take control of building your resilience, better able deal with setbacks, and eager to consume all the feedback that comes your way, to enhance your performance potential.

CHAPTER 16

Decoding Resilience in Sales – Myths and Realities

How many times have you heard these statements thrown out in your sales career, particularly over the last couple of years?

- 'Just be more resilient, and roll with the punches'
- 'You need to be resilient to be successful in sales'
- 'Have a positive mindset'

Endlessly, I'm guessing. But what does it actually mean to be resilient? How can we work on it proactively? Saying 'just be resilient' is about as useful as telling someone to 'calm down.' It never works, and often makes things worse.

Before we get into the component parts of resilience and how to build it, it's important to address four of the predominant myths associated with it. These often cause confusion, impact our mindset and ironically make us feel less resilient.

The 4 Myths of Resilience

Myth #1: Resilience is a personality trait that some people naturally possess

No one is 'naturally' resilient. The people you may perceive as naturally resilient have probably been through a number of experiences, in their career and personal life, that have helped them develop tenacity. Research by the academic Ann Masten suggests that rather than being an innate trait, resilience can be developed through life experiences.[15]

If you consider yourself naturally resilient, you may have had experiences in your childhood that built that capacity, but you may not be consciously aware of the connection.

Here are some examples of situations in life that can build one's resilience without them being aware of it:

- Growing up in a turbulent family environment or experiencing divorce
- Coping with family conflicts and developing conflict resolution skills
- Taking on responsibilities at an early age due to family circumstances
- Navigating through discrimination, prejudice or social exclusion
- Adapting to a new culture, language or environment
- Dealing with rejection in relationships, friendships or professional settings
- Facing financial difficulties and learning to manage limited resources
- Coping with the loss of a loved one or experiencing another significant personal tragedy

One factor that can play a part in the perception of being naturally resilient, or particularly self-confident, is what you learn or adopt from your parents or primary caregivers.

Having a conversation with them or other family members about this can help you understand where some of your resilience may come from.

Labelling someone as 'naturally' equipped with some attribute only creates a limiting belief that we can never reach that level, and leads to a fixed mindset of not working on developing it.

Instead, remind yourself that resilience is something you can work on, and although life experiences can help us develop it, there are also actions and perspectives that can do so over time.

Truth #1: Resilience can be developed over time through experience and knockbacks.

Myth #2: Resilience is about always being strong

There is a perception that resilience equals strength. The problem with this mindset is believing that we should never let anything bother us, which means we end up bottling up thoughts and feelings. Research indicates that true resilience involves emotional regulation and adaptive coping mechanisms. Psychologists Susan Folkman and Richard Lazarus suggested that the way we interpret or react to an event can have a more powerful impact on our stress level than the event itself.[16]

For example, someone might try to avoid showing that missing a target hit them hard, act like they didn't want that promotion in the first place, or hide their disappointment when a valued colleague leaves the company. All of these responses that can lead to unresolved thoughts and feelings that can negatively impact their future performance and wellbeing.

There's danger in believing it's 'the opposite of strength' when we let these things get to us. With this perception,

we can see ourselves as weak, self-judge and pressure ourselves to feel a certain way.

Resilience is really about being flexible and adaptable.
It's not about never being knocked down. It's about knowing what to do when that happens, and having the tools
that help you get back up.

It's being able to address those situations head on, process and reflect on what you have learnt from them and how
you feel. This then gives you a better understanding of what
to do in the future or what solutions to go looking for.

Scenario	The resilience-is-strength myth	Resilience is about being flexible and adaptable
Missing a target	Hiding disappointment, being anti-social in the office or jealous of colleagues. Trying to keep busy, and taking your frustration onto calls.	Sharing frustration with your manager, focusing on the pipeline and what you can control, change or keep doing for the next quarter.
Breaking up with a partner	Act like it hasn't affected you, focus on all their flaws, avoid processing it and take the weight or unresolved issues into the next relationship.	Reflecting on what you learnt about yourself in that relationship, finding a friend to speak openly with, and becoming clearer on what you want from the next person you meet.
Not getting a promotion	Acting like you didn't want the promotion in the first place, and bottling up disappointment that can turn into resentment of your job and company, impacting your performance and stress levels.	Share your disappointment with a colleague or manager, seek feedback on the reasons and use it as guidance on what to work on, while using the setback as fuel to seek promotion in the future.

Truth #2: Resilience is about being flexible and adaptable.

Myth #3: Resilience is about never giving up

Having grit – that sturdy mix of courage, resolve and strength of character – can be a valuable asset in life. But, it can harm us when the right response might be to change direction or avoid the pursuit altogether. If you try to exemplify this unwavering fortitude with everything, you can end up chasing lost causes, wasting time and energy, and detracting from other promising deals or productive prospecting.

This may be the case with that one stubborn deal that sits in your pipeline, with an ever-changing forecast, which you insist you'll close if you just spend more time on it. This leads you down a road of neglecting other opportunities that are more likely to come to fruition.

Sometimes this feeling of having true grit can come down to pride, and wanting to be seen as never giving up on things. But it can also be linked to the Sunk Cost Fallacy, a theory espoused by behavioural economists Daniel Kahneman and Amos Tversky.[17]

The Sunk Cost Fallacy is a cognitive bias where individuals continue investing in a decision or project based on the resources (time, money, effort) they have already committed, despite the current and future costs outweighing the benefits. You've sunk a lot into it, so it may feel important to continue plugging away, but it's time to read the writing on the wall.

We let past investments influence our present decisions, even when those expenditures are unrecoverable. That deal that's been languishing in your pipeline, that you feel you can't let go of, could be needlessly burning fuel that should be directed into other deals.

True resilience involves knowing when to persevere and when to step back. It's being conscious of where you should best spend your time and energy. Knowing when to pull back and change direction, even though it can be frustrating. Or, when to step back from going out of your way for a colleague who never tries to help themselves, in order to protect your own sense of resilience and wellbeing. Or, perhaps, when to acknowledge that the position you're in isn't right for you, despite the efforts you've made to learn and grow, since the culture and environment aren't healthy for you.

Truth #3: Resilience is about knowing when to persevere and when to step back.

Myth #4: Being resilient is just about you

Resilience isn't just about being able to personally withstand stress and adversity. It's also about how we respond to others when they're facing difficulties. Social support plays a crucial role in resilience, as highlighted by research showing the buffering effects of interpersonal relationships on stress. Psychologists Sheldon Cohen and Thomas Wills argued that large social networks are associated with positive outcomes, such as health and wellbeing.[18] In sales, this means being mindful of how we interact with our customers and colleagues during challenging situations.

Of course, you need to take care of yourself first and foremost, but it's also important to consider others. Remember that our reactions to setbacks can have a significant impact on the people around us, and that we have a responsibility to maintain a collaborative, supportive attitude.

For example, let's say a customer is unhappy with our product or service. It's natural to feel defensive or frustrated, but it's important to approach the situation with empathy and a willingness to listen.

By acknowledging their concerns and taking proactive steps to resolve the issue, we can turn a negative experience into a positive one, and even build stronger forward-looking relationships.

Similarly, when a colleague is facing a challenge, we can offer support and encouragement to help them through it. Even if that same experience is something you've handled well and have never struggled with, be mindful that not everyone will find it quite so easy.

This might mean lending an ear, perhaps mentioning how you used to grapple with this and how you responded, sharing helpful resources, or simply offering a kind word of support.

By being a source of strength and support for others, we not only help them overcome their challenges but strengthen our own resilience in the process. Another valuable outcome from this is that you build a collective culture of resilience.

	Individual culture	**Collective culture**
Scenario	Nearly half the team members are new, or have underperformed year-to-date.	
Response	Everyone focuses on themselves; little guidance or support is offered across the team.	Those who've developed resilience/performed well support those who are new or missed a target, offering advice, tips and assistance.
Outcome 1	Some individuals leave, others continue to struggle, and there aren't any real lessons learnt.	This gives these individuals encouragement, guidance and lessons to work on, as they build their own resilience.
Outcome 2	The collective environment becomes quite bleak, and even those who are performing well find it less enjoyable to work in.	The team dynamic strengthens and the work environment is more healthy and enjoyable for everyone.

Even when things don't directly impact you due to your better-developed level of resilience, it always pays to consider others around you, as that can influence the wider work environment and how things turn out for everybody.

Truth #4: Resilience is also about considering others.

Number	Myths	Truth
#1	A natural trait that only certain sales people possess.	Can be developed over time through experience and knockbacks.
#2	About always being strong.	Being flexible and adaptable.
#3	Never giving up on situations.	Knowing when to persevere and when to step back.
#4	It's all about you.	About considering others too (once you've taken care of yourself).

Inspirational Insights

Louis Kwakye, Group CRO at Perkbox & Vivup, a consolidated health, wellbeing, benefits and rewards services provider, perfectly sums up this resilience myth:

"We all win when we can look left and right and know we all care, are focused and have the right purpose."

I met Louis a few years back through a networking group, and worked with him and his team while he was at the employee engagement platform Reward Gateway.

He's been pivotal in creating a healthy, successful culture in the business, and this outlook is one of the reasons behind that. Looking at collective resilience is something that's often missed when considering workplace culture.

Even if you're not in a leadership position, you can still contribute to shaping collective resilience.

Your Three Key Takeaways:

1) Resilience is something we can develop over time, not necessarily something we're born with or a natural trait only a percentage of people possess.

2) Being resilient doesn't mean we should never be affected by disappointments, but rather adaptable to them and how we get back on the right track.

3) Resilience doesn't mean never stopping, it's about knowing when to step back and when to push on, while also considering others around yout.

CHAPTER 17

The Five Ingredients to Developing Resilience

To further understand and be able to build resilience, it's important to recognise the characteristics that contribute to it. A bit like baking a cake, when you understand the individual ingredients required, you have a better understanding of how to make it.

There are five characteristics of resilience, as detailed by researchers Adam Smith, Brian Jones and Celia Brown, which I'll cover below.[19] Becoming familiar with them will provide greater awareness of which areas you've developed to a good degree and others you'll want to work on.

When reading through these, think about tools that have already been covered in this guide, which can support you in developing specific aspects of resilience. And at the end of this guide you'll find The Playbook, with a section dedicated to resilience and these five characteristics, including guidance on which tools to use to work on them.

1. Challenge

It can sometimes feel like certain knockbacks or moments you experience in your career and life are tough to overcome. Those who have a good level of resilience view setbacks or difficulties as challenges to overcome rather than insurmountable obstacles.

This perspective fosters a mindset that seeks growth and solutions in the face of adversity. In the context of working in sales, this characteristic can manifest in the following ways:

Scenario	Low levels of resilience: Challenge	High levels of resilience: Challenge
Lost deal	Takes a lost deal personally, becomes demotivated, and hesitates to pursue new prospects.	Sees a lost deal as a learning moment, adjusts strategy and channels energy into pursuing new opportunities, with renewed energy.
Tough customer feedback	Takes the feedback personally, feels discouraged, and may shy away from future client interactions.	Sees the input as constructive, acknowledges areas for improvement, and uses feedback to enhance performance, remaining open to client communication.

Inspirational Insights

I first became aware of Melanie Mills, CRO at Caxton Payments, a Fintech service provider, through Making Moves, a London-based networking group for women in tech sales. Below, Melanie shares how she's handled challenges in her life.

"Challenges, in my opinion, make or break you, and if handled effectively they can propel you forward," she told me. "Every failure or disappointment is a lesson to be learnt and builds an extra layer of resilience.

"One pivotal knockback for me was the realisation that my own business was coming to an abrupt end just as I was turning 30. For some reason, being that age was very important to me, a real milestone. I imagined I'd be a millionaire! I had to reevaluate my life, and after seven years of owning my own business I had to make a huge step backwards to be able to move forward again.

"Ultimately the lessons learnt gave me a better understanding of the businesses I then worked for in the future. My dream failed, so I reset my sights, made plans and moved forward at a fast pace, to compensate for lost time, taking everything I learnt into my future career. What doesn't break you makes you stronger. You just have to focus on adopting a new perspective to help understand these challenges, build your character and make you who you are today.

"From developing this mindset, my career has gone from strength to strength. I fast-tracked, travelled the world, and there was nothing that wasn't possible. From the option of moving to New York, to buying a property, to meeting my daughter's father, when you're happy and fulfilled, everything else falls into place.

"You are in control of your own destiny, and while there will be setbacks, it's how you pick yourself back up to fight another day. Don't think you have to do it alone, either. I chose to take as much help as possible from counselling, mentors, training, and selected true and critical friends to support that progress."

2. Commitment

Having clear goals in your personal life and career provides you with a roadmap that guides your actions and decisions. These goals (your hospitals) – which we can characterise as commitments – serve as a constant reminder of what you're striving for, anchoring you during challenging times.

Resilience is closely tied to commitment because resilient individuals maintain a steadfast dedication to their objectives, regardless of obstacles they encounter along the way. This commitment acts as fuel that propels them forward, even when faced with setbacks or difficulties. Overleaf are some examples of this:

Scenario	Low levels of resilience: Commitment	High levels of resilience: Commitment
Establishment of a new annual target	Feel overwhelmed by the long-term goal, questioning your ability to achieve it and motivation to stay at it. This could lead to a lack of enthusiasm, making it challenging to set and pursue ambitious targets for the year.	Being mindful of personal long-term goals you're working towards, what you'll learn from this new financial year, and breaking down sales targets into manageable milestones. Therefore, approaching the year with a determined and optimistic mindset, staying focused on your personal goals as well.
Challenging month	Might consider giving up on short-term goals. The challenges may lead to frustration and a questioning of why you're even doing this job.	Reminds you of the reason you are doing what you're doing. Have a number of goals outside of work you're building towards, providing greater perspective, and not seeing the challenging month at work as a catastrophic setback.

3. Personalisation

An important ingredient in resilience is being able to avoid taking everything personally. Being able to recognise that not every situation or reaction from another person is because of you helps avoid overthinking things and allowing them to bother you.

This also involves being able to determine what is within your control and recognising/accepting what isn't. In sales, this characteristic can be exemplified as follows:

Scenario	Low levels of resilience: Personalisation	High levels of resilience: Personalisation
Prospect doesn't reply to an email	May internalise the lack of response, feeling personally rejected or questioning your communication skills. This could lead to self-doubt and hesitation in future outreach.	Understand that the lack of response may be due to various external factors. Don't take it personally, analyse and adjust your approach as needed, and continue outreach confidently, recognising that individual responses aren't indicative of your personal worth or skills.
Rude customer on the phone	May take the rudeness personally, feeling hurt or offended. This could impact your confidence in dealing with other customers and lead to a negative emotional carryover to subsequent calls.	Recognise that the rudeness of one customer is not a reflection of your own worth. Remain professional, empathetic and resilient, not letting this single negative interaction affect your overall approach to customer interactions.
Change in business direction	Become increasingly frustrated by the change, focusing on things you can't control and coming to resent it. This then impacts your performance and how you come across to colleagues.	Even though you may not understand or accept the reasoning, accept that you can't control it. So, adapt to the change, align your strategies with the new direction, and contribute positively to the evolving business environment.

4. Permanence

When faced with challenges, you can sometimes perceive a state of permanence, sure that how you feel or think now is how you always will. Resilience here involves seeing negative events as temporary, rather than enduring setbacks, and recognising that things can improve. In sales, this characteristic can be demonstrated in the following ways:

Scenario	Low levels of resilience: Permanence	High levels of resilience: Impermanence
Missed target	See it as a permanent failure, leading to self-doubt and a belief that future targets are unattainable.	View the missed target as a temporary setback, learn from the experience, and remain optimistic about achieving future targets by adjusting strategies and maintaining a long-term perspective.
Economic downturn impact	Believe things will always be this tough, and success is unobtainable, leading to loss of motivation and focus, along with questioning your career.	Adapt to economic challenges, understanding the temporary nature of downturns, and actively focuses on what's in your control, not only in the present, but how to set yourself up for when things change (building future pipeline).

5. Pervasiveness

Some setbacks or obstacles you face in your day may have a domino effect on your evening, weekend or with other people. Resilient individuals prevent negative events from affecting unrelated aspects of their lives. Here are some examples of how this can look:

Scenario	Low levels of resilience: Pervasiveness	High levels of resilience: Non-pervasiveness
After a tough morning of cold calls	Carry negative emotions throughout the day, affecting interactions with colleagues, other tasks and future cold calling sessions.	Compartmentalise the tough morning, recognising it as a specific challenge. Maintain confidence in overall sales ability, adapt strategies for the afternoon, and approach subsequent calls with renewed focus, preventing the negative experience from affecting the rest of your day.
Demo doesn't go to plan on a Monday	Might let the disappointment pervade your outlook. Carry the frustration into subsequent meetings, and even let it affect your perception of the entire work week and things at home.	Isolate the setback to that specific demo. Recognise it as a singular event, use the experience to refine your approach, and tackle the rest of the week's demos with a fresh and optimistic mindset, preventing the negative impact from spreading across the entire work week and into your personal life.

Psyche Success Stories —
Emily & Overcoming Pervasiveness

Meet Emily, a Customer Success Manager working for a scale-up sales engagement company. Emily faced a significant challenge in her role: she tended to let a tough customer call in the morning impact the rest of her day.

The negative reactions and stress from the initial difficult interaction would pervade her mindset, affecting her confidence, performance and mood, and she'd often take that feeling home with her.

We started working together on this, and focused on the concept of pervasiveness and how it was influencing her thinking. One tool that we focused on was the Five Senses Exercise.

After a challenging call, Emily began implementing the exercise, a mindfulness technique covered in the previous section, which helps bring attention back to the present moment. By doing so, she aimed to reset her emotional state and prevent the lingering effects of negative emotions throughout the day.

The results were transformative. Emily found that by incorporating the Five Senses Exercise into her routine, she was able to compartmentalise challenging experiences without allowing them to hijack her day.

This newfound resilience allowed her to approach subsequent calls with a fresh perspective. Rather than dwelling on earlier challenges, she learnt to extract valuable lessons from difficult interactions while maintaining a positive and proactive disposition.

As a result, Emily not only improved her ability to handle challenging situations, but also enhanced her overall performance in customer engagements.

Activity D1 —
Resilience Reflection

With the tools discussed in mind, note down in the first column which area of resilience you feel is your strongest.

Then, in the second column, indicate which 1-2 areas you'd like to focus on.

You'll be able to find the specific tools and ways to work on each part of resilience at the end of this book.

Areas of strength	Areas to focus on

Your Three Key Takeaways:

1) Focusing on the specific characteristics of resilience will help you develop yours more effectively.

2) Your levels of resilience can be quite different in your work and your everyday life.

3) Focus on a specific area you want to work on (perhaps based on the Resilience Quiz) and create some tangible actions to follow.

CHAPTER 18

From Setbacks to Success – How to Turn Failure into Fuel

I want to address the word failure. It's often misused, particularly in sales. It comes up when a call doesn't go to plan, you don't get a promotion or you fall short of hitting your target.

Something only really becomes a failure when, after bumping up against an obstacle, you stop trying and give up altogether. But if you dust yourself off and stick with it, you've merely encountered a setback. By definition, a setback is an event that delays or reverses some of the progress you've made. It is not necessarily a definitive, hard-stop fail.

In this chapter let's refer to those rejections, deflating problems and vexing delays as knockbacks.

In the realm of sales, knockbacks show up in many different forms. They're an inherent part of the journey to success. Any high-performing salesperson, leader or founder will tell you that those experiences along the way shaped who they are.

Knockbacks in sales teach us resilience, adaptability and the art of overcoming objections. They push you to reevaluate your strategies, refine your tactics and approaches, and develop a deeper understanding of your customers' needs and concerns.

Yet, despite knowing that they are part and parcel of being in sales – that we'll see them regularly and they can be great lessons – these inevitable knockbacks can still impact and hinder us.

Knockbacks can leave us questioning whether we're good enough, and if we'll ever be capable of hitting our target again. But when viewed in the right way, these disappointments can be stepping stones towards growth and improvement.

One of the ways to achieve this is by acknowledging that not all knockbacks are created equal. I would suggest that you're likely to encounter three types.

When we lose out on a deal, a call goes sideways or we get passed over for promotion, it can really hurt. We can resort to blaming uncontrollable things 'out there,' finger-pointing and disavowing any responsibility for what transpired. Or, at the other extreme, we can assume all the blame, and really beat ourselves up for what went wrong.

Five-time world chess champion Magnus Carlsen warns that viewing all knockbacks as identical can lead to wasted energy on uncontrollable aspects of our lives, and hinder learning from these experiences.[20]

Instead, Carlsen outlines three distinct types of setbacks:

1. **Preventable Knockbacks:** These are unfortunate turns that, on reflection, you had prior knowledge of and the ability to prevent. These typically occur when an approach or idea was counter to a proven process. This can sometimes come down to a lack of training or rein-forcement of the process.

Examples of these could include:

› Sharing the wrong pricing with a customer
› Ignoring an email format you've been asked to use
› Going into a customer call unprepared
› Not researching a prospect sufficiently
› Not changing 'Hi, First Name' in a generic email template before hitting send

When finding yourself in these situations, it's important to recognise and acknowledge your mistakes in a constructive way, to ensure that you ultimately learn from them.

Scenario	Unconstructive	Constructive
Heading into a call unprepared and having things go poorly.	Going through the 'should have/would have/could have' cycle, questioning what you did and didn't do.	Deciding never to take a call for granted; scheduling ample prep time before the next one; carefully noting what went wrong.
Not modifying a generic email template before sending.	Obsessing over why you didn't pay attention to personalizing the email salutation.	Making sure you start carefully reading through draft emails before sending.

It's easy to get caught up in the past and judge yourself for it. When we overanalyse the past and ruminate on it, our primal brains replay it as if it's happening right now, thinking we can somehow change the outcome.

Unconstructive self-criticism only creates more angst and frustration, and takes the focus away from what you'll do next time. Forward-focused reflection helps ensure that you acknowledge the lesson and take steps to avoid it happening again.

Doing this also prevents the negative 'what ifs' from taking up residence in your head. You can end up obsessively dwelling on whether the next call will go like the last one.

2. **Complex Knockbacks:** These occur when you've prepared all you can, and taken steps to address countless eventualities, but new, unexpected or uncontrollable combinations of factors arise.

   Examples of these could be:
   › A prospect having to move the meeting
   › Budget cuts in the customer's business
   › A change in regulations in the sector
   › Unpredictable global events (war, COVID-19)

These unavoidable knockbacks can feel the most frustrating, because you'd done your best to be prepared. But in these instances, it's important to avoid thinking you could have somehow controlled or changed an 'Act of God.'

If you don't identify these complex knockbacks, it can lead to needlessly changing your controllables, such as your sales process or question structure, when these weren't factors that led to the problem.

The key here is to stand firm with your controllables and avoid overthinking the need to change everything.

Nonetheless, you may find that there were some controllable factors you could have handled differently to avoid this. In some cases, this seemingly inevitable obstacle could become an avoidable one and if that's the case, refer to the process of how to deal with preventable knockbacks.

3. **Intelligent Knockbacks:** These are the types of stumbling blocks where you learn something new from the experience. That learning could be about yourself, a process/approach, or how others respond. Here, a bit of experimenting is necessary. This is where the entrepreneurial idea of 'failing fast' comes from – the notion that the quicker you work through things that *don't* work, the sooner you'll get to what does.

   Examples of this include:
   › Launching a new product
   › Starting in a new job or being promoted
   › Entering a new territory or market
   › Presenting/cold calling for the first few times

   This type of hindrance is vital to building resilience and avoiding a fixed mindset. It's important to reflect on the process here, what you learnt from it, and what you'll continue on with, change or stop doing in the future.

   This idea of a knockback as a learning experience is particularly useful when bringing new employees into a job or when you are starting one. It can be tremendously helpful to encourage learning from their disappointments and embracing them, rather than fearing them.

Inspirational Insights

Morgan J. Ingram, Founder and CEO of the marketing firm AMP, is a great example of how to look at these hurdles. I came across Morgan on LinkedIn a few years ago and loved his videos and perspective. I invited him onto my podcast, and we've done several episodes together.

Morgan started out as an SDR, and in his initial three months fell short of hitting quota. The phones were a battlefield, emails went unanswered, and his social media selling tactics were met with silence. It was a tough pill to swallow.

In the face of adversity, he caught his breath and took a step back, realising there was more he could do to level up.

This missed target became a turning point. He immersed himself in sales development, studying it with newfound intensity. A key piece was focusing on the things he could control, rather than dwelling on what he couldn't.

Life, he realised, throws challenges our way, and victory lies in our ability to uncover solutions. Every week became a study session in self-improvement. Cold calling, email canvassing, presenting — each skill was dissected, learnt and applied. The more Morgan invested in mastering the craft, the sharper he became in his work. The key, he discovered, was taking incremental steps towards greatness.

Morgan put these learnings to use, and with a refined approach saw his confidence surge, more meetings were booked, and he made his numbers the following month. He went on to a string of successes, eventually becoming one of the top sales reps in the company.

The lesson: The only real defeat is in throwing in the towel, not in the temporary setbacks themselves. Embrace the journey, learn and persevere. As Morgan came to realise, success awaits those who refuse to quit.

The more salespeople feel they need to avoid any type of knockbacks, the more likely they are to stick to what they know and be less inclined to push themselves. That's detrimental from a personal perspective, and dangerous for a company, as it prevents evolving and adapting to the market and world.

Recognising and understanding the different types of knockbacks allows us to approach them in a constructive and productive way. We can learn from our own mistakes or lurking unknowns, acknowledge uncontrollable circumstances and use them as opportunities to grow and improve, as individuals and organisations.

Next time you're faced with a knockback in your career, consciously label it as one of these three types and decide what actions you can take to move forward. The aim here isn't about stopping unfortunate knockbacks altogether, as a lot are uncontrollable, but rather controlling how you respond to them. Along with this, it's not saying you should always be happy and welcoming of knockbacks, but to recognise once they've occurred there is always a lesson in there somewhere to reflect on and take forwards.

Activity D2 —
Defining Your Three Types
of Knockbacks

With these three varieties in mind, think about some of your own experiences with each and go through the table below. Try and pick one situation for each type, identify what made it that variety, and note what it taught you or reaffirmed.

Knockback	What was the situation?	What made it this type of knockback?	What did that help you do differently or realise?
Preventable			
Complex			
Intelligent			

Inspirational Insights

Tom Glason, Cofounder & CEO of ScaleWise, which connects growth strategy experts with high-potential businesses, has an insightful story of taking lessons from your knockbacks. Tom and I crossed paths initially via LinkedIn and I've always enjoyed listening to and reading his insights, so I was thrilled when he said he'd contribute to this book.

Tom grew up in Asia, moving to the UK in the bleak winter of 1987 when his parents divorced. He was forced to quickly adapt to the culture and harsh weather while also trying to get his head around his parents living separately.

He found established groups of friends hard to penetrate, his sister went 'off the rails' and his dad became an alcoholic. Along with these challenges, Tom's early career didn't have the best foundations.

"I had the worst boss you could imagine when I was in my early 20's," he told me. "I was in an enterprise sales role, selling seven-figure deals, but my sales manager was under a lot of pressure, as the team was not hitting targets.

"She became a micromanaging bully who was intent on undermining me at every opportunity. It ended up massively affecting my mental health, my sleep, my relationships and ultimately led to me being signed off with stress.

"Once I left the company, I realised that something good needed to come out of the situation in order for me to move on and bounce back. I first needed to recognise that the situation wasn't about me, my ability or my worthiness. It was about my boss, her own self-esteem and the pressures she was under.

"Then the most powerful shift in me came, when I decided to use the experience to motivate myself to become the best boss anyone could have. I was determined to be the opposite of my awful boss, and when I took my first VP Sales role I was acutely aware of how my actions and behaviours would impact others. I used my old boss as a driving force for a lot of my decisions.

"I took back complete control of what was a really awful situation for many months. When I got my first leadership position, I was deeply motivated to be the best boss that I could be. This translated into having a highly-engaged, motivated and high-performing team."

"The moral of the story is that although, in the moment, it may not always instantly feel like it, there is learning, growth and progress that comes from every setback or 'failure.'"

Your Three Key Takeaways:

1) Failure only occurs when we give up on something. If we can learn from it and continue on, then it is simply a setback we can ultimately benefit from.

2) Not all knockbacks are the same. When faced with one, be mindful of identifying it as either the preventable, complex or intelligent type.

3) The more we embrace these and focus on falling forward, not backwards, the sooner we can build on them and acknowledge that they are a key component of our success.

CHAPTER 19

Mastering the Art of Receiving Feedback in Sales

We've all been that situation – whether in a one-on-one session, an email or a customer review – where you hear the words, 'Can I give you some feedback?' Or, it might take for the form of, 'I thought this was great, but ..."

This is enough to strike fear into many sales reps, and even seasoned managers. Your ego steps in and metaphorically covers your ears as your defence mechanism switches on. The ego gets a bad rap, but it's there to protect your self-esteem and it often gets involved when your primal brain jumps in.

Going into defence mode, you feel the need to justify yourself, and make excuses, in the face of what's been said.

All the while, you're not really listening and taking in the information that the other person's sharing with you. You may recognise some of these initial responses to feedback:

- The reason I did that was because ...'
- 'I don't believe that's right.'
- 'I said that because I thought it would ...'

Feedback is often something we fear because it can be quite a reactive response. Very rarely will we ask for it. It's often something we're given unexpectedly, or when we perceive that we've done something wrong.

Of course, leaders and your company's culture can create a constructively supportive environment where you're given feedback when you've done things well, not just when you haven't.

Without feedback, we don't grow or develop. And we often continue doing the wrong things, over and over again. That is the very definition of insanity.

So, how can we become better at receiving feedback? How do we put ourselves into a position of listening to that person, and ensuring that we understand that they feel heard and we benefit from the feedback?

Let's focus on two things related to this. First, there's a useful four-stage process we can employ.

Step 1: Listen to understand and summarise back

We've all heard some version of that advice. Listen well, in order to understand, and then respond with an affirmation. Micro-listening combines both of these elements. When someone's giving you feedback, listen to it, but also take in what they're saying with the intention of playing it back to them.

Before we get into this, it's important to note that you don't necessarily have to agree with the feedback somebody's offering up. That's not the point. But you want to be certain you've understood their perspective. For example:

- 'Just so I'm sure, what you're saying is that I need to work on X. Is that right?'
- 'I want to clarify what you said. What you'd like to see more of from me is ...'
- 'OK, let me check I've got it. You're frustrated because ...'

In doing this, you achieve a couple of things. First, when you're listening with the intention of having to convey a summary of the message back to that person, you're using the rational part of your brain to take in the information, which stops your primal brain from getting involved.

This reflects the principles discussed in organizational consultants Douglas Stone and Sheila Heen's book, *Thanks for the Feedback*. They emphasize the importance of active listening and summarizing, to ensure understanding and reduce defensive reactions.[21]

This is where the ego sits and where self-preservation stories are created – you start to think the feedback is a personal affront, that it's just not true, and that you need to justify yourself. By listening with the intention of summarising back, you don't allow this part of your brain to activate.

Second, when you play the message back to that person, they feel completely understood, or feel that they might need correct themselves. For example, they might say:

- 'That's it, you characterised it perfectly.'
- 'Correct. And I would add that ...'
- 'No, that's not what I meant. What I was trying to say was ...'

If you accurately summarise it, the person feels understood and listened to, which is the most important thing. If you've misinterpreted it or they've miscommunicated, they can then flag it, which prevents you from going down a road you never needed to walk.

The worst thing we do when we receive feedback is try to come back with a justification of our original position. They won't feel heard, you don't feel heard, and it goes round in circles.

Once you've effectively summarised the feedback, and it's been acknowledged, you're all ready to move onto the next step.

Step 2: Thank the person

Perhaps your manager has shared some thoughts following a call you led, or a colleague commented on an interaction you'd had the previous week. Offering thanks might feel like the last thing you want to do if you don't entirely agree with their feedback or don't truly understand it yet. But a simple expression of thanks is important. It could as simple as:

- 'First of all, thank you for sharing that with me.'
- 'I appreciate you coming to me to talk about this.'
- 'Thanks, this is really useful to know.'

Saying thank you is an effective way of disrupting the primal brain and embracing the feedback. It allows your rational brain to engage and look at it logically, rather than as an unreasonable personal attack. It also demonstrates that you appreciate the person's thoughts, views and opinions.

Beyond that, it opens the door to them conveying feedback in the future. The worst thing you can do is seem ungrateful for someone telling you something. They're then unlikely to share an observation next time, but they're still going to think it, which means that nothing changes and the relationship suffers.

A person has taken time to reflect on something relating to you and tell you what they think about it. So, appreciate that, even if you don't feel comfortable doing so straight away.

Step 3: Ask to probe

What you want to do here is to ask to enter the conversation, and use this step when perhaps the feedback isn't clear. You may not have been given specific examples, or you don't truly understand it. This is as simple as something like:

- 'Can I ask you a couple of questions to better understand what you mean?'
- 'Will you give me a bit more on where you think this is showing up, so I can work on it?'

It's a constructive way to dive in – the most likely answer you'll get is 'yes,' and you'll be on the same wavelength. You're asking questions. You're not trying to defend yourself here. You're not trying to justify things. You're seeking to understand where this feedback is coming from.

Step 4: Probe to understand

Just like you would with a prospect or customer, here you want to ask a series of questions to get clarity on that feedback. The more questions you ask, and the more effective they are, the better you'll understand the feedback before you jump in. And again, the person will feel like you're trying to really understand them.

Here are some questions you might want to ask:

- 'How would you deal with this if you were in my shoes?'
- 'Could you give me a couple examples of what you meant by that?'
- 'Next time this happens, how would you suggest I approach the situation?'
- 'Are there any suggestions or recommendations you have for addressing this?'
- 'Can you give any additional insights or perspectives that would help me better understand?'

Psyche Success Stories — Nora, Learning to Embrace Feedback

Nora, a pre-sales solutions architect, faced a significant challenge in her career. She consistently found herself getting defensive when receiving feedback from her manager and colleagues. She became increasingly uptight about the input, hindering her ability to genuinely absorb and constructively apply it. Not only were the same issues coming up, but based on her reaction, her colleagues became less willing to give her suggestions and try to help her.

Nora raised this as a concern in our one-on-one sessions. After working through the four-step approach referenced above, she started to more actively listen, and summarising feedback to engage her rational brain and avoid defensive reactions. She became more mindful of thanking those giving the feedback, and looked to understand the comments and how they could benefit her.

Nora's systematic application of these steps transformed her relationship with feedback. She shifted from a defensive stance to a proactive and open-minded approach, welcoming feedback as an opportunity for growth. Her success in utilising it not only contributed to her individual development but also fostered a positive feedback culture within the team.

Activity D3 —
Being Curious With Feedback

Think through the scenarios below, have a look at the sample responses, and write down questions you could use to probe and better understand this sort of feedback (Step Four).

Feedback scenario	Ask to probe	Probe to understand question example	Your added question
You've been told you need to prioritise your time better.	'Thanks for sharing. If it's OK, I have a couple questions on how I can achieve this.'	'What's one thing that worked for you when you were in my position?'	
A colleague gives you feedback on an email you sent.	'I appreciate your thoughts on this. Mind if I ask a couple of questions to understand how to improve?'	'Which parts of the note do you think are the strongest?'	

Taking these steps in response to feedback means you're more likely to welcome it, understand it and utilise it. All feedback is a matter of perception, and through these steps you'll either uncover a blind spot to work on or address a misunderstanding.

This will serve you well in the long run. If and when you find out that someone misinterpreted something you've said or done, you can clarify it, and everyone can move on to more productive things.

Your Three Key Takeaways:

1) Summarising and repeating the input back to the other person engages your rational brain, ensuring that you avoid going into defensive mode.

2) Always acknowledge and thank someone for sharing feedback. They'll generally be doing it with good intentions.

3) Be curious about the feedback you receive, asking questions to better understand it. It can help uncover a blind spot or clarify a misunderstanding.

CHAPTER 20

The Value of Proactively Seeking Feedback

One of the most effective ways to become more comfortable with feedback is to go looking for it. As mentioned above, the reason we can get defensive is that it can come as a surprise in situations where we're not expecting or prepared for it.

By asking for feedback, we feel more in control, because we've initiated the conversation. That means we're less likely to get our backs up, with our primal brain jumping in.

Being proactive in asking for feedback can also open the door to receiving it more frequently. As with any other aspect of your job that benefits from repetition over time, receiving regular, ongoing feedback will help improve your performance. That applies to unsolicited input as well as feedback that you request — the more you receive it, the more familiar, comfortable and helpful it can become.

There are three things to work on to become more effective at seeking feedback:

1. Seek Feedback, Not Constant Reassurance

When looking for feedback, it's important to avoid having it become a need for constant reassurance, due to self-doubt. There's nothing wrong with seeking positive affirmation, but when it becomes constant, and a sign of second-guessing yourself, this can negatively impact you.

It stops you from forming your own opinion and stunts the growth of your confidence.

Of course if you're brand new into a role or company, there will be aspects of reassurance that you'll want to gain initially, but just ensure that it doesn't become a unhealthy habit over time.

2. Share Your Perspective

To ensure you avoid an over-dependence on reassurance, share your perspective, up front, when asking for feedback. By doing this, you also show that you've put some thought into it.

Plus, you then have a yardstick to start with, to help validate or gain a different perspective on subsequent input. This over time builds your self-belief, as you aren't just asking others for feedback, and going with their suggestions or guidance. You're cultivating your own, based on varied source material.

3. Be Specific With Your Questions

You may have some winning questions you ask your prospects and customers, but what about with your colleagues or manager when seeking feedback? Often I see people asking ineffective questions, or ones that are too broad, such as 'Can I have some feedback?' or 'How does this sound?'

These queries can result in unhelpful, woolly answers. When asking for someone's input, be specific.

With the previous three points in mind, here are some examples of effectively soliciting feedback.

Ineffective feedback question	Effective feedback question
Am I doing this right?	What are your thoughts on my approach to this? I'd be happy to share my perspective on it too.
Do you think this would work?	Here's why I'm going to try this. How do you think that would resonate?
Does this look good?	I worded the note this way because I want to show that I understand their issue in the market. Do you think it captures the customer's situation?
What's working for you at the moment in your role?	You seem to plan your time really well. I'm trying to tighten up on that. Can you take a look at my diary and share any thoughts on how I've planned my week?

The final aspect of being more proactive with requesting feedback is about looking and sounding open to receiving it. Of course, it's your manager's job to give you feedback, but input can also be useful from colleagues, other leaders, customers, prospects, friends, family and your partner.

You might think you're being proactive and casting a wide net in asking for feedback, but still come across as closed off or defensive in the way you do so.

Be conscious of the tone you're using and your body language. For example, avoid crossing your arms or looking like your body is doing the opposite of being open to thoughts and suggestions. Sometimes it's helpful to add disarming statements, such as:

- I want you to be as honest as possible. I'd really appreciate it.'
- 'Give it to me straight; no need to dress it up.'
- 'Seriously, I won't take it personally. This will really help me.'

These statements are priming your brain for embracing feedback and signalling that you want to hear it, meaning your primal brain doesn't feel like it needs to get involved. If you're subconsciously telling yourself you want to hear something, you won't shy away from it.

Activity D4 —
Seeking Feedback

Over the next seven days, give yourself the challenge of asking three different people for feedback.

Using the box below, write down the three people you want to get input from. Look for a mix, perhaps tapping a manager, colleague, customer, friend or partner.

1. Write down 1-2 questions you want to ask.
2. Make note of the feedback and what you gained from the conversation.
3. Finally, reflect on and jot down how you felt about the process.

When doing this, remember the four-step approach from the previous chapter: listen and summarise back; thank the person; ask to probe; probe to understand. It can be useful to actually tell the other person you're practising using that methodology, as a way to improve on how you solicit, receive and process feedback.

The person	What 1-2 questions do you want to ask them?	What feedback did you receive?	How did it feel to proactively ask for input?

Inspirational Insights

Judy Moon is VP of Market Development and Strategic Sales at Digimarc Corporation, a provider of intellectual property identification and authentication services. I've heard her speak at some events, and she's always had a real focus on remaining curious, seeking feedback and leaning along the way.

Judy was an immigrant from South Korea, having moved to the US with her family when she was a child. A decade after taking time off to raise her children, she re-entered the workforce and built an entirely new career in the tech sector, drawing on all her experiences.

This required an immense amount of curiosity, seeking feedback and learning as much as she could while doing the job. She recognised that the more input she sought, the more she could learn new things and take on new challenges. To that end, she's passionate about leveraging technology to solve problems for a better world.

Judy's advice to us all: "Always be curious and keep learning."

Action to embed habit: Accountability is a great tool to rely upon when looking to implement a new habit. Tell your manager or a colleague that this is something you're working on, and encourage them to ask you every two weeks about some new pieces of feedback you've proactively gathered.

Your Three Key Takeaways:

1) The more you seek feedback, the more comfortable you become with it. You can continuously use it to make improvements or reinforce what you're already doing.

2) When asking for input, avoid having it become a need for constant reassurance. Share your perspective first and be specific with your questions.

3) Be sure that you're conscious of looking and sounding open to receiving feedback when seeking it.

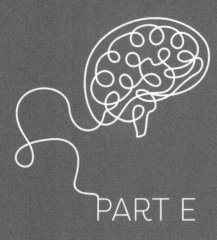

PART E

Unleashing Your Inner Sales Champion

Developing a healthy mind for peak sales performance isn't just about reframing your thoughts and emotions, or how you handle setbacks. It's also about how you become your own biggest champion. We've already discussed the impact and importance of being more conscious of our self-talk, and the limiting beliefs that can stem from it.

Becoming more mindful of your own self-worth, which makes you great at what you do and who you are, not only reduces the frequency of those limiting beliefs, but builds your confidence and self-belief. And with that, you can continue to grow in your career, while maintaining a healthy mind.

If you aren't conscious of this, you'll find yourself in a constant race of comparison, feeling behind where you 'should' be, concerned that you're not doing 'enough' in your professional life, and somehow not adequate in general.

This can impact your confidence in going for a promotion, speaking up in team meetings, building your personal brand and, most of all, never truly acknowledging your success or the progress you've made.

In this part of the guide, we'll delve into the unhealthy habit of comparing yourself with others, and how to increase your self-belief. We will also look at 'imposter syndrome,' and how to address it. Alongside this, you'll gain a better understanding confidence, the power of self-reflection and creating healthy, productive comparisons.

After all, it's great to receive recognition and feedback from others, but for us to become the best version of ourselves, we want to be our own biggest supporter. Not in an arrogant way, but fully knowing what we're capable of, giving ourselves credit when we deserve it.

By doing this you can waste less time and energy on toxic comparisons, instead channelling effort into your own personal development and advancement in your sales career.

CHAPTER 21

Understanding the Two Types of Comparison in Sales

First, comparison is a fundamental aspect of human nature. It is impossible to avoid comparisons with others in life. That's especially so in sales, where clearly defined comparative metrics are a constant presence. When used in a healthy manner, comparison can serve as a great motivator.

For example, seeing colleagues performing well can be quite inspiring. It shows that it's possible for you to achieve the same levels of success, and that everyone can be 'winning' at once.

However, if not consciously managed, we can slip into constant unhealthy comparisons, added stress, jealousy, hopelessness and frustration. You can start to obsess over colleagues doing well, and having a sense of resentment seeing them closing deals or getting a shout-out.

Before delving into how to utilise comparison in a healthy way, let's explore why we frequently find ourselves comparing ourselves to others. Social Comparison Theory, initially proposed by psychologist Leon Festinger,[22] argues that we cannot define ourselves independently, but need to evaluate our worth by comparing ourselves to other people.

There are two types of social comparison:

1. **Upward social comparison** occurs when we hold ourselves up to individuals we perceive are superior to us in some way. They might be a top performer or inspiring manager in our company, or a person we follow online.

    This kind of comparison can be helpful, as it provides inspiration and motivation to better ourselves, gives us a benchmark to work towards or instils a sense of hope.

    On the flip side, however, this upward comparison can become unhealthy, causing you to feel like you'll never reach that level. This can lead to feelings of despair and a lack of motivation.

    Here are some examples of scenarios you may recognise, and the differences between unhealthy and healthy upward social comparison.

Scenario	Unhealthy upward social comparison	Healthy upward social comparison
A colleague closes a big deal with a new product you launched this year.	You focus on them being 'lucky' and feel a sense of jealousy towards them.	You're pleased for them, and see it as a good sign that you can potentially achieve the same.
You have someone in the team who is a top performer.	You feel that no matter what you try, you'll never be as good as them. You're reluctant to ask what they're doing to achieve this.	You use them as constant inspiration or healthy competition, to keep your performance at an optimal level. You enjoy learning from them.
You follow a person on LinkedIn who has a great personal brand and generates consistent social media engagement.	You compare yourself to them, and how much more successful they are than you with their online content. You find this frustrating.	You always enjoy reading their content, take ideas from them for your own posting and are pleased for them.

2. **Downward social comparison** takes place when we compare ourselves to individuals we believe are worse off than us. This might happen when we see a colleague lose their job or is underperforming.

This form of comparison is usually aimed at boosting our self-esteem or cultivating a sense of gratitude for what we have that others may not.

The other side of downward social comparison is that it can potentially lead to worries about you ending up in the unenviable situation you've observed.

Here are some examples that highlight the differences between unhealthy and healthy downward social comparison.

Scenario	Unhealthy downward social comparison	Healthy downward social comparison
Someone you're connected with on LinkedIn is made redundant.	Start thinking you could end up like this, which can make you anxious and cause you to lose focus in your role.	Express empathy and offer support if you know them well enough. You appreciate the position you're in, and what you've done to get there.
A colleague missed their target for a couple of months.	Begin thinking you will miss your target in the next quarter, and start overly focusing on the uncontrollables.	You acknowledge what you're doing right, and remind yourself that if you keep at it, this won't happen to you.
A co-worker is struggling to grasp a new product pitch.	Start second-guessing your own knowledge and approach on the new product, even though there's no evidence to suggest there's a gap.	You may offer them tips on how to better understand it, while also recognising that your pitch and product understanding are serving you well.

Inspirational Insights

Doreen Pernel, Chief Sales Officer at cloud computing provider Scaleway, has some very honest reflections and thoughts on this topic. I met Doreen a few years back when she invited me to run a webinar for her team on limiting beliefs. I then went on to support her team while she was working at artificial intelligence platform Dataiku.

I've always admired Doreen's openness, and have seen how highly regarded she is by her colleagues and employees. Here are some of her beliefs:

"It's true for any subject: it is unhealthy to compare yourself to others, but even more unhealthy to go through this process while being promoted.

"I remember my first promotion to second-line manager, and managing managers. I pretended to be 100% confident, to be 100% in the game, and I gave it my all to achieve our goals and targets. We did, but I didn't succeed alone.

"I'm lucky to always be surrounded by a great team, and the first thing I do when getting in a new team is to work on our alignment, strategy and sales culture.

"While doing this, in my private life, I was showing more vulnerability. Showing vulnerability in sales isn't common, but I now tend to show more vulnerability to my direct team and express that it's OK to be vulnerable. It shows that you're human. To show your humanity in sales, in leadership, in your private life, will only bring greatness!

"Ultimately, don't try to do it all alone. No one is asking you to be a superwoman. Your partner, your family and friends are your village. And it's the same in sales; it takes a village to close a deal! Together, you'll make it."

To Doreen's point, comparison — and an altogether human sense of vulnerability — can be a common thing to feel at any stage of your career. Surround yourself with others, talk, be vulnerable with those you trust and avoid bottling up those thoughts.

In their healthiest form, both upward and downward social comparison can serve as a powerful tool for self-improvement. When we compare ourselves to others, we can identify areas in which we can develop, and also appreciate what we have.

The next question becomes what we can do to ensure that we build healthy and productive comparison habits in our sales role. This all starts with reframing the way you look at external comparisons.

Your Three Key Takeaways:

1) There's no escaping comparison in sales. It all comes down to what you use that comparison for.

2) In its healthiest form, comparison can spark motivation, give you hope and increase your gratitude for what you already have.

3) Recognising which of the two types of comparison (upward or downward) you experience the most helps you focus on what to work on.

CHAPTER 22

Reframing Your Upward Social Comparisons

External upward social comparisons are a vital part of developing a healthy, high-performance mindset in sales. However, it comes down to how you're using them. We've discussed the healthy and unhealthy versions of upward social comparison. One way to develop the healthy sort is to shift how you view that upward social comparison, your self-talk and the thought process surrounding it.

Our brains are wired to constantly scan for potential threats. With every interaction we have with another person, we're trying to establish if they're a friend or foe. Whether it's a prospect, new team member, manager or colleague, your brain is searching for signs and signals of where this person sits in the social hierarchy.

When we constantly compare ourselves to others, such as top performers or someone who's just been promoted, we build an unhelpful perspective. This entails the following sorts of thoughts:

- 'They got so lucky with that deal.'
- 'They're just naturally good at cold calling.'
- 'I'll never be able to get the numbers they do.'
- 'They always seem to be so confident when presenting.'

Going down this rabbit hole, our brain starts to see them as foes. This can trigger feelings of envy, jealousy and unhealthy upward social comparison. I often hear salespeople say, 'When I saw that person close a deal, I have to admit, I felt envious of them.'

This stems from remaining in a static comparison mindset without exploring what we admire about that person, and how we can develop those qualities ourselves.

As noted previously, a key reset to help build a healthy, high-performance mindset is reframing statements into questions. Let's take that negative self-talk above and reframe it, as follows:

Unhealthy comparison statement	Reframed as healthy comparison question
They got so lucky with that deal.	What controllables did they focus on in that deal, and how did they deal with the uncontrollables?
They always seem to be so confident when presenting.	What is it that I like about the way they present, and how could I learn more about it from them?
I'll never be able to get the numbers they do.	What are 2-3 things within their control that they do each month to stay consistent with their performance?
They're just naturally good at cold calling.	I want to know how they became so good at cold calling. What could I ask them about that?

What do you notice about these reframed questions? First of all, by asking them with the intention of learning from the other person, and even approaching them for guidance, our brain begins to perceive them as less of a threat and more as a friend or asset.

And, as a theme we've been developing throughout this guide, they also give our brain direction, and something to work on and solve, rather than a statement to sit on, allowing it to grow and fester.

Doing this not only leads to creating healthy comparisons in your mind, but also gives you the questions to solve, helping you continue to develop and build that growth mindset.

Along the way, focus on becoming more aware of the value of having success around you. To that end, which of these places would you rather work in?

1. No one in the sales team is hitting their target or advancing professionally.
2. You have colleagues nailing their numbers and being promoted.

I'd like to think you'd want to be part of that second group, who you could learn from, feel inspired and motivated by, and join on an upward trajectory. The other environment certainly wouldn't be conducive to learning, growth, success and happiness.

Recognising the value of having people succeeding around you can help reframe your self-comparison with others. That success, when looked at in a constructive way, gives you inspiration and access to knowledge from those achieving it.

Psyche Success Stories — Ben Reframing Upward Social Comparison

I had Ben, an Enterprise AE, come to me a couple of years back for help on unhealthily comparing himself with colleagues and those he followed on LinkedIn. Ben had achieved a couple of internal promotions, but after he'd moved into enterprise selling, he saw deals taking much longer to close.

He wasn't getting that regular dopamine hit from having one opportunity after another close, and began to resent colleagues celebrating wins. He started thinking he would never be as consistent as them.

Ben was regularly posting content on LinkedIn, but had seen a dip in engagement. Others he followed were doing well in that regard, which also fired that sense of jealousy.

This all had him dwelling on so many things he couldn't control about others, and his own circumstances, leading him to feel stressed and increasingly frustrated.

Through my coaching work with Ben, he began to focus on reframing his comparisons. First, he acknowledged that it didn't make sense to compare himself with sellers outside the long-sell-cycle enterprise space, who would naturally be closing the smaller deals more frequently. He also started becoming more open and intentional about talking with colleagues who did similar work, and engaging with a professional networking group. This helped him better understand what he could actively control and develop.

He became more open-minded about asking top performers what they were doing to build urgency. At the same time, he started taking inspiration from those he followed on LinkedIn, picking up ideas on how they structured their content and analysing what worked. He even requested a call with one of them to better understand this, and adopted new ways of freshening up what he posted.

As a result, Ben started to see better LinkedIn engagement, including a few viable leads. He was no longer judging himself compared to dissimilar types of sellers, and became more consistent in developing his skills.

Activity E1 –
Reframing Comparison

Write down some of your own statements that could be seen as unhealthy and not serving you well in your role. Then, think about how you can reframe them into healthier questions that serve you better.

Unhealthy comparison statement	Reframed healthy comparison question

For help in developing a healthy version of downward social comparison, I'd recommend revisiting the insights and tools we went through earlier, for exploring and validating limiting beliefs. This will help you filter through irrational beliefs and avoid jumping to conclusions about situations without considering other possible scenarios.

Avoiding Unhealthy Online Comparison

In recent years, we've all become more mindful of what we eat and drink, and their impact on our physical, mental and emotional wellbeing. However, we can often overlook our digital consumption.

The content we engage with daily can significantly influence how we perceive ourselves, and where we stand in life and work. Scrolling through LinkedIn on our lunch break, TikTok on the commute to work or Instagram before going to bed, we're constantly measuring ourselves against what we encounter online. This can make us feel inferior, convinced that we're behind where we 'should' be.

It pays to be mindful of the content we consume and ask whether it inspires or intimidates us, leaves us in a better place or makes us feel worse off.

What we see online may look incredible, but it doesn't always reflect the reality of what is going on. When you see a carefully curated snapshot of someone's life, polished up for maximum effect, and compare it with the reality of your work-a-day world, that's bound to not go well.

Social media can be addictive, and bingeing on content that makes us feel like others are doing better than us can be fertile ground for limiting beliefs, sapping our aspiration and motivation. At its worst, it can lead to self-loathing, anxiety and even depression.

Inspirational Insights

Back to Sean Hayes at Aircall, who we talked about earlier, for his perspective on why it's important to set intentions when using online platforms like LinkedIn:

"The Sales Development Representative role is often the first job out of university, for those that went, and so we always have a young crop of talent in our team," he told me. "For many, there's a lot of uncertainty in this period of life. Many SDRs, however convincing they are in the interview process, fall into sales. Yet, they still find themselves comparing themselves to their peers.

"Even top performers fall victim to this social comparison. One SDR called me after she had hit her target with two weeks to spare in the month and said she wanted to quit sales. I dug a little deeper, and it turns out that a friend from university had posted a picture of her new Mercedes on LinkedIn, so now she wanted to be an accountant like her.

"My first bit of advice would be to always approach LinkedIn with intention. If you find yourself in the habit of scrolling aimlessly, you're likely going to be impacted negatively by the updates on your feed.

"Most salespeople use LinkedIn for outreach, so if you go there for this reason, ensure that you set goals you hope to achieve. And, set a limited amount of time to do this in. It's OK to go onto LinkedIn to check on status updates, but be sure you do this at the right time for you and your mindset."

That's a great piece of advice from Sean, as it can be easy to see updates and posts online, instantly lose your perspective and feel like you're behind or should be doing better. Be intentional with what you're doing on these digital platforms and what you want to consume.

Activity E2 —
The Social Cleanse

When was the last time you audited your social media accounts? Set a reminder to do this with some regularity. Here are a few pro tips:

1. Choose one platform, whether it's TikTok, Instagram, or LinkedIn.
2. Scroll through, asking yourself for each piece of content:
   - Does this person inspire or intimidate me?
   - Does it make me feel like I can apply what they're doing to my own life and benefit from it, or does it make me feel stuck or further behind?
3. If it's the latter, unfollow that content.

Your Three Key Takeaways:

1) Reframing external upward comparisons involves shifting from a statement mindset to asking questions for learning and growth.

2) Unhealthy comparisons, often through social media, can be mitigated by setting intentions and being mindful of what you consume. This can create a shift to more productive comparisons.

3) The sooner you can look to learn from someone, and get clear on what you appreciate about them, the sooner you'll see them as valuable, and less as a competitor to be unhealthily fought or feared.

CHAPTER 23

Building the Habit of Internal Comparison

A key factor driving us to invest too much time on external comparison is a lack of internal comparison. We noted that comparison is in our nature, and the human brain will automatically look for equivalencies in every situation. If we haven't cultivated the habit of internal comparison – looking within ourselves – the mind will always look externally.

Plus, without that consistent internal comparison and reflection, we won't be able to recognise or acknowledge progress we've made, which means we'll always look at others and believe we're lagging behind or not doing enough.

Even with the healthiest form of external comparisons, if we aren't aware of our own progress or where we stand, we won't be able to utilise them effectively.

For example, you could reframe those external comparisons in a healthy way based on what you admire about a colleague's cold calling skills or consistency in performance. But if you don't have a benchmark of where you stand or have progressed in this area, you won't find the information as useful. The first way to address this is to focus on building the habit of self-reflection.

The Importance of Self-Reflection

Salespeople and leaders often ask me for the most effective ways to cultivate a healthy and high-performance mindset. I always include building the habit of self-reflection. It's a vital component of developing self-awareness, self-esteem, a growth mindset and reducing dependence on external recognition.

Self-reflection enables us to look back and contemplate our thoughts, feelings, emotions and actions. It provides a valuable opportunity to appreciate how far we have come.

Just like tracking a run or bike ride on an app to assess performance and give ourselves a sense of accomplishment, self-reflection allows us to evaluate the time and energy we invest in our work, which typically amounts to 40-70 hours a week.

By engaging in self-reflection, we acknowledge that even if we haven't reached our peak, we're likely much further along than we were a week, a month or a year ago.

Without this practice, not only do we end up creating unhealthy external comparisons, but we can become overly reliant on external recognition and constantly seek validation. And then, when recognition is not received, we may doubt ourselves or feel that we've done something wrong, leading to a mindset of constantly needing to prove ourselves.

Additionally, without self-reflection, external recognition quickly loses its impact, and we may struggle to believe it is genuine.

Here are some examples of useful questions to ask yourself when you self-reflect:

1. How am I better off compared to this time last week/ month/year?
2. What achievement am I most proud of from last month?
3. Which aspect of my life can I show more kindness towards this month, and how can I do that?
4. What insights have I gained about myself or my team this past month, and what areas might I need to work on?
5. How can I utilise these insights to make progress this month?
6. What one thing do I want to stop, start and continue doing this month to develop myself or my team?
7. Looking back at the month, what could I have done to feel satisfied?

You can ask yourself one or two of these questions at the end of each week. Personally, I dedicate 10-15 minutes every Friday, near the end of the day, to think through Weekly Wins. I reflect on the things I'm proud that I accomplished, focusing not on external events but on my own actions and efforts.

One of my favourite questions to ask is, 'How am I better off compared to this time last week/month/quarter/year?'

Asking this question regularly is beneficial for any aspect of your life, but particularly in specific areas of your role that you're working on. For instance, you can reflect on how you've developed your cold calling skills over the past week, month or year.

Take the time to play back a customer call and evaluate your progress. I've applied this approach to various podcasts, and discovered that over the years I've improved in areas such as avoiding filler words, being more mindful of my questions and refraining from talking over guests.

Self-reflection doesn't just help you acknowledge progress, it also helps create more awareness of what's working in your approach. This reinforces what was discussed in the Surfer Mentality section of the guide. When you are more aware of what's working for you in your role, the more consistent and intentional you can become with it. This helps create a sustainable and consistent approach to your sales performance.

This is not about disregarding setbacks or challenges you faced during the week, or more long-term ones. It's about finding balance, dedicating specific time to recognise the progress you've made and building the habit of self-reflection.

Moreover, remember that self-reflection extends beyond work. Acknowledge achievements in areas such as exercise, diet, personal development, networking, socialising and the family dynamic.

Activity E3 —
Your Weekly/Monthly Wins

Spend 5-10 minutes thinking of your answers to the following questions, and jot them down in the adjacent box.

How am I better off compared to this time last week/month/year?	
What achievement am I most proud of from the past month?	
Which aspect of my life can I show more kindness towards this month, and how can I do that?	

What insights have I gained about myself/ my team this past month, and what areas might I need to work on?	
How can I utilise these insights to make progress in the month ahead?	
What one thing do I want to stop, start and continue doing this month to develop myself or my team?	Stop: Start: Continue:
Looking back at this month, what could I have done to feel satisfied?	

Action to embed habit: Put 10-15 dedicated minutes in your calendar each Friday afternoon to consider your Weekly/Monthly Wins, to become more aware of your progress, and what you're noticing as a result.

Keep Track of Your Success

Along with self-reflection, another way to focus more on developing your internal comparison is keeping a track of your success. Receiving an uplifting email, Slack shout-out or positive verbal feedback from our manager make us feel good. But these moments can quickly fade into distant memories amidst the fast-paced nature of sales and life.

Particularly during challenging times, it's important to regularly reflect on these moments. This helps us maintain balance and prevents us from creating a negative narrative that undermines our mindset, progress and overall wellbeing.

To ensure that you have easy access to these moments, I recommend creating a 'success folder' on your computer. Whenever you receive feedback from a prospect, customer, colleague or manager, make a note of it in this folder.

Cultivate a habit of reviewing the feedback, perhaps every couple weeks, to remind yourself of your achievements and strengths. This can also serve as a go-to resource when you're in a slump, feeling off, and self-doubt starts to creep in.

Your success folder could include:

- Emails from customers (closing a deal, acknowledging your support)
- Feedback (from your manager, colleagues, performance reviews)

- Shout-outs (via email or group chats)
- A LinkedIn post that mentions you

During difficult periods, it's easy to forget about all the positive things you're doing and the strides you're making. Consider this folder a montage of your greatest hits – a collection that can rejuvenate and reorientate you.

Even when things are going well, it serves as a valuable source of additional motivation and recognition for the time, effort and expertise you invest in your work, and the positive things that flow from that.

Activity E4 —
Creating Your Success Folder

Before moving on to the next chapter, take a few minutes to give this a go. Create your own Hit Parade folder, cataloguing recent successes.

1. Open a new folder on your computer.
2. Copy in positive, reaffirming emails/messages/comments you can use to reflect on.

Make a habit of proactively looking back on this material every few weeks, as well as on those days where you feel like you're under a wave (per the Surfer Mentality).

Your Three Key Takeaways:

1) The more you focus on your own progress and journey, the less caught up you'll be in comparing yourself with others.

2) Celebrate your journey through self-reflection. You might not be where you want to be yet, but you're probably further along than where you were.

3) Track your success and on the tough days, when you begin doubting yourself, revisit it to remind yourself of everything you've done well.

CHAPTER 24

Focus on Courage, Not Confidence

Think about how often you hear these kinds of statements:
- 'Just be confident.'
- 'Confidence is key.'
- 'You need to be confident to be successful.'

While confidence is undoubtedly important in the world of sales, its source and development are often misunderstood. It's not just something you can decide to have at a moment's notice, and switch on when it's needed. There are two myths associated with confidence that cause many salespeople to focus on the wrong things. Let's get into them.

Confidence Myth #1: It's a natural ability that some people possess.

First, the idea of natural confidence is a myth, just like the natural-born resilience fiction we discussed earlier. The same principles apply here, about genetics and the perception of it, so I won't repeat myself. But let's summarise:

Confidence is not something you are born with. It's tempting to look at colleagues, leaders or people on LinkedIn and assume they are naturally confident.

Rather, it's a skill that can be developed by anyone, and it can take various forms. Being the loudest or having the biggest presence in the room does not define confidence. You can even make an argument to say this is sometimes a form of masking.

Buying into the concept of natural confidence can create a limiting belief that no matter how hard you work on yourself, you'll never be as confident as those around you.

This belief alone can negatively impact your confidence levels. We, of course, have different baselines of certain attributes in our lives, confidence included. But no matter who someone is, where they come from or what sort of persona they project, they'll have had to work on their confidence. It doesn't come by accident.

Truth #1: Confidence is a skill that everyone can develop over time.

Confidence Myth #2: It is always needed in new situations to be successful.

Another fallacy is that confidence is required in every situation. We often hear phrases like 'Just be confident' when approaching new or unfamiliar situations, such as cold calls, demos, pitches or negotiations.

As we've said, this is not something you can simply switch on. It flows from taking action and doing something.

Telling yourself that you need to be confident in something you've never, or rarely, done will either make you feel less self-assured because you believe you're missing something, or prevent you from taking action altogether, leading to procrastination.

This mindset can also create an element of permanence – as we discussed regarding resilience – where without factoring in the context of the situation, you will feel you'll never be confident enough, leading to limiting beliefs around this. For example, this can stem from statements like:

- I'm not confident with cold calling (Context: having just joined a company in an outbound sales role).
- I'm not confident in running a demo (Context: having just been promoted to an AE).
- I'm not confident in public speaking (Context: never had regular opportunities to do it in previous roles).
- I'm not a confident manager (Context: having just been promoted).

All of these statements leave you in a static headspace, short-circuiting your brain's ability to effectively overcome these hurdles. Context is key here. Of course you're not going to be confident in something you've done or had little exposure too.

Instead, look at confidence as the outcome of doing something repeatedly. You may not have it when starting something new, but by doing anything enough, whether it's cold calling, managing or presenting, you'll develop it over time.

Think about the analogy of baking a cake, and see confidence as the cake itself, instead of an ingredient like flour. Every time you attempt to make that cake you'll improve upon it, and over time it'll be something you can consistently create.

Truth #2: Confidence is the outcome of doing something repeatedly, learning from the experience each time.

So, if you shouldn't focus on expecting to be confident in new situations, what should you do?

Instead of expecting confidence to miraculously show up in new or unfamiliar situations, focus on looking for courage. Mustering courage is something you can control, and it can be applied in every new situation.

Unlike confidence, courage does not burden you with heavy expectations when facing something new. The more courageous you are, the more confident you will become.

The braver you are about making cold calls, the more confident you'll become in doing them. The braver you are about standing up and presenting in front of people, the more confident you'll become as a result.

Courage also gets you to focus internally on what you can control. Confidence, when you don't feel it, often causes you to unhealthily compare externally with those that do.

By consistently putting yourself in new situations, you'll gain confidence and learn how to navigate them effectively.

Here are some examples of how you can reframe your view on confidence:

Initial statement	Reframed statement
I'm not confident about cold calling (having just joined a company in an outbound sales role).	By making more cold calls, I'll become more confident in my ability to do them effectively.
I'm not confident about running a demo (having just been promoted to an AE position).	By observing others and being courageous about leading a demo, with someone showing me the ropes I'll become more confident in them.
I'm not confident about public speaking (never had regular opportunities to do it in previous roles).	By finding small moments, like a team meeting or internal training, to talk or present, I can build my confidence in talking to larger public groups.
I'm not a confident manager (having just been promoted into that role).	By building stronger relationships with my team, understanding them and networking with other managers, I'll become more confident in my management abilities.

Inspirational Insights

Shelley Lavery, Cofounder and CCO of Jiminny, a coaching and conversation intelligence platform, is always a joy to speak with. She's got that kind of energy that lifts you up, but is also very honest and open about life. She always tells it like it is, and has a real authenticity about her.

A fun fact about Shelley is that at the age of 14 she became a black belt in karate, after training twice a week for seven years. Although she didn't realise it at the time, the accomplishment shaped her into the person she is today.

"I remember crying my eyes out in the toilets, with my mum there, because I was scared," she says. "I'd watched others go through this hellish experience for a black belt, being beaten up by multiple people. But despite that fear, I really wanted to do it!

"That's when I first realised you can be completely frightened of something and still want to do it. This has served me so much over the years, from leaving jobs, moving to New York, stepping away from relationships and starting a business with my partner Tom.

"Yes, all these things carry a risk with them, but it doesn't mean you shouldn't give them a try. Don't be afraid of those feelings — it's OK to have them, but they can also be signs that this really matters to you. The main driver behind the decisions I've taken in my life and career comes down to wanting to feel alive and, to be honest, just f**t it, life is too short to wonder *what if.*"

But even with this go-getter outlook, it doesn't mean things have been easy for Shelley. There have been funding challenges, headaches with managing investor relationships, times when it's felt like the business was slipping away. But something she told me she's thought about throughout is this: "The more grazed knees you get, the more you remember they don't last that long."

She says a pivotal thing that changed along the way, and has made all the difference, is her high-level perspective on life.

"I used to get wrapped up in that feeling of anxiety when things would happen, struggling to be present, and it would impact my judgement. I feel more centred now, avoiding getting too high with the high moments or too low with the low moments. If I was to speak to my younger self, I'd really emphasise taking perspective when things happen. Which, I get it, isn't easy. There's an element of having to go through these experiences to realise that, but even asking yourself in the moment, will this really matter next week, month, or in a few months' time?"

Activity E5 —
Acts of Courage

Think about something you're wanting to build your confidence in (a hobby, work role, public speaking, etc.). Ask yourself what 1-2 ways you can be courageous in this week. It could be signing up for a challenge, making a tough call you've been putting off, sharing something in a team meeting.

Jot some of these ideas down below, and perhaps even share them with someone to add that element of accountability.

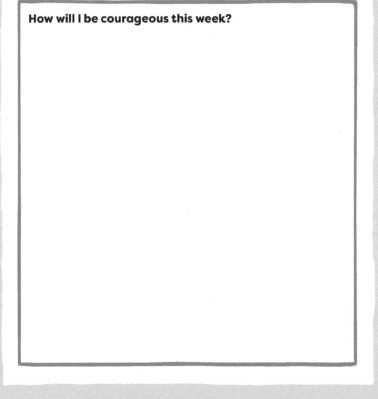

How will I be courageous this week?

Your Three Key Takeaways:

1) Confidence may not be something you're naturally gifted with, but it's an attribute that everyone can develop over time.

2) Confidence is the outcome of doing something repeat-edly, learning from the experience each time.

3) Developing your confidence comes from being courageous.

CHAPTER 25

The Four Types of Imposters

Have you ever felt like you aren't good enough for your role? That perhaps you don't deserve to be paid the amount you're earning? Or that your company or customers will eventually realise you're just winging it?

If so, this could be a sign that you've experienced Imposter Syndrome. This is a psychological experience where you doubt your abilities, feel like a fraud, and believe that your achievements are a result of luck or external factors rather than your own competence.

It's completely normal to feel this way at times, especially in a competitive, target-driven environment like sales, where the pressure feels constant.

Let's start by identifying some signs that may indicate Imposter Syndrome, in yourself or others. As we go through these, ask yourself how applicable they are to you:

- An inability to realistically assess your skills and competence.

- You look for validation in senior figures or peers and see their opinion as the sole factor in whether you're successful or not, despite experience in the area.
- When you achieve success in familiar situations, you attribute it to luck or describe it as a fluke.
- Berating your own performance, constantly finding the smallest things to be critical of.
- Fear that you won't live up to the expectations of others, despite being in a role or situation for a good amount of time.

To better understand the syndrome and how to work on it, it's important to break it down into key elements. The academic Valerie Young, an expert on this dynamic, has flagged four main types of imposter one can perceive oneself to be.[23] Note that some people can be a mix of several or all of these.

#1 The Expert

As this imposter, you constantly feel the need to possess all the knowledge and information, never satisfied that you know enough. Despite others perceiving you as the go-to person for answers, you still experience insecurity about your expertise. Belief that you're this type of imposter can cause you can delay starting something because you think you need to gather all the information first, leading to procrastination.

You also constantly worry that someone, be it a prospect, peer or manager, will ask a question you can't answer, which fuels a fear of shame. As a result, you approach every situation with the need to prove yourself, and miss out on learning from others because asking a question feels like a sign of weakness.

Examples:
- Avoiding pitching a new product feature until you've read literally everything about it and crafted the 'perfect' presentation
- Everyone comes to you for product knowledge, but you wonder why, and assume it's out of convenience or because you've been there the longest
- Trouble admitting to a customer that you don't know the answer, instead trying to sidestep it or be vague, worried that they'll judge you if you say you need to go and find out

#2 The Perfectionist

This is the most well-known type of imposter, often wearing their compulsion as a badge of honour. The perfectionist imposter sets impossibly high self-expectations that are difficult to reach. This proclivity constantly tells you that you're not doing enough or are falling behind in life, without clearly defining what 'enough' means. When you fail to meet a goal, you experience significant self-doubt and struggle to let go after making a mistake or saying something you regret.

You may exhibit micromanagement tendencies in both your work and personal life, and find it challenging to delegate tasks to others. This imposter tends towards excessive overthinking, regretting past actions, procrastination and anxiety when starting something new.

Note that if this imposter persona's perfectionism inspires you to strive for bigger goals, that's a healthy side effect. If it makes you feel stressed and anxious while reaching for that goal, or even at the mere thought of achieving it, then this is unhealthy perfectionism.

Examples:
- Planning out every last detail of a presentation, but when the requirements change a few days before, you lose all rational thinking and instantly assume it's not going to go well
- Taking every setback personally, thinking a disinterested prospect was rude because of something you did
- Despite overall great feedback from your manager, only focusing on the single area for suggested improvement, and judging yourself for not recognising it already

#3 The Natural Genius

This imposter feels that if they're truly competent in their role, they should always excel effortlessly, without the need for extra effort, training or learning. If you require any of this, this persona convinces you that it's because you're not good enough, rather than acknowledging that the task was difficult or required external support.

This imposter tendency often leads you to give up easily when trying new approaches or hobbies, avoiding challenges at work and being hesitant to share that it took a while for you to understand or accomplish something. It keeps you within your familiar zone and promotes a fixed mindset, preventing you from putting yourself forward for promotions or exploring new, fulfilling experiences.

Examples:
- Reluctant to learn from others in the team, fearing they'll judge you first for asking, and again if you aren't able to instantly grasp the new knowledge
- Avoid pushing yourself for stretch objectives, as they require extra effort, which you feel should come naturally, so you stick to the basic targets and goals
- Doubting your abilities and thinking your manager doesn't have faith in you because they suggested a training workshop, rather than acknowledging that they're encouraging you to continue to learn and grow

#4 The Workaholic

The workaholic imposter convinces themself that they'll never be as knowledgeable or talented as those around them. This compels them to work harder than others, putting in more hours and energy. If you're driven by this tendency, you derive self-worth from being seen as busy and become anxious when you can't visibly display your busyness, such as working remotely.

This imposter type experiences stress and anxiety when not working, and feels the need to be first in and last out of the office. You constantly seek out new responsibilities, even when you already have a full plate, which leads to added stress. Asking for help becomes difficult because you want to be perceived as capable of managing everything.

A person with this predilection is in a continuous state of stress and a prime candidate for burnout, continually challenged by the thought of switching off from work and being fully present in non-work moments.

Examples:
- You find yourself feeling chronically unsettled over the weekend, struggling to disconnect from work
- Neglecting spending time with your friends or partner because you're putting in long hours at the office, or are too exhausted after a long week to socialise
- Saying yes to whatever comes your way at work, meaning you're unable to make time for your own work and overcommitting

The Four Types of Imposters

#1 The Expert	#2 The Perfectionist
• Feels uncertain about level of knowledge despite being a go-to person • Procrastinates, fearing they forever need more information • Worries about not having all the answers and avoids asking questions • Examples: Avoiding pitches until perfect, assuming others only ask your advice out of convenience, evading spotlight situations	• Sets impossibly high expectations; never feels they've done enough • Experiences self-doubt and anxiety over mistakes and feedback • Micromanages and struggles with delegation • Examples: Overplanning, taking knockbacks personally, obsessing over minor negative feedback
#3 The Natural Genius	**#4 The Workaholic**
• Believes competence means excelling effortlessly • Gives up easily, avoids challenges and sticks to familiar zones • Hesitant to share learning processes and avoids new experiences • Examples: Reluctant to ask for help, avoids stretch goals, sticks to well-worn routine	• Believes they must always work harder because they'll never be as knowledgeable or capable as others • Derives self-worth from being busy; struggles to switch off • Takes on too many responsibilities and avoids asking for help • Examples: Anxious when not at the office, neglects social life, overcommits at work

Activity E6 —
Identifying Your Imposter

1. Using the first box below, jot down which examples you can relate to from the four Imposter Syndrome personas.
2. In the second box, note which of these four personas you feel you can most relate to. (Include a mix if you identify with multiple types.)

Imposter Syndrome examples

Which of the types of imposter can you relate to?

Identifying these personas is an important first step in dealing with your inner imposter. Becoming more aware of the signs will help you notice them when they're occurring, and acknowledge that it's your imposter that's present.

I think it's important to mention here, that it's not the behaviours on there own that signal a sign of potential Imposter Syndrome, but rather the intentions behind them. For example, feeling like you want to keep learning, do a great job or want to put a good amount of time in to things aren't inherently bad or an instant sign of Imposter Syndrome. But if your intention of doing these things is driven by fear or stress, it can be linked to Imposter Syndrome.

When it's not Imposter Syndrome

Imposter Syndrome can be one of the primary blockers to becoming our own biggest champion. But let's address a misunderstanding that I see among many sales reps and leaders. People can misdiagnose a case of this syndrome when they in fact have a real deficit of skills or a learning gap.

There are situations where these feelings of uncertainty and self-doubt might be a valid reflection of your lack of experience or insufficient understanding of the job. For example:

1. **Genuine lack of experience or skills.** A salesperson may be in a new role or situation where they lack certain abilities or insights, such as cold calling, industry knowledge or presenting. Over time, much of this can be dealt with through training and from exposure to these aspects.

2. **Performance feedback.** If a salesperson consistently hears that they're performing below expectations, the self-doubt they experience may be a reasonable response, rather than unwarranted Imposter Syndrome.

This isn't to say both can't be the case at once, but it's important to reflect before jumping to the assumption that it is Imposter Syndrome.

To sum it up, Imposter Syndrome is when despite having experience, skills, knowledge and success in a role or situation, you still feel like a fraud and attribute any upside to luck.

Conversely, when you lack relevant experience, knowledge or capabilities, but feel like a fraud and attribute any success to luck, this isn't necessarily Imposter Syndrome, but a legitimate skills, knowledge or training gap.

Activity E7 —
Imposter Syndrome or Skills Gap?

Here are some questions to ask yourself to establish which of these you're experiencing:

1. Is what I'm doing brand new to me, or have I experienced this a number of times?
2. Has it been suggested that I work on this specific area, or is the 'need to improve' feedback coming exclusively from me, to myself?
3. Am I doing everything in my control to give myself a chance of succeeding in this situation?

Your Three Key Takeaways:

1) There's nothing wrong with experiencing Imposter Syndrome. If you do feel it or have done, you are not alone.

2) Being mindful of the four types of inner imposters can help you pre-empt their negative influence when they're likely to show up.

3) It's not always Imposter Syndrome you're experiencing; it could be a legitimate skills gap or reaction to a new situation you've never faced.

CHAPTER 26

Leveraging Your Imposter Syndrome in Sales

Imagine this scenario: You and your friends are discussing holiday plans, and each of you has different opinions and perspectives on what a good holiday looks like. You can clearly distinguish your own suggestions from those of your friends. You can separate your perspective from theirs.

Name Your Imposter

Naming your imposter works in a similar way. By giving it a name, you are able to separate it from your own identity and thoughts. Without naming your imposter, you and your imposter's thoughts merge together, making it challenging to find a clear, rational, effective way forward.

Naming your imposter allows you to spot it when it starts to interfere, and enables you to address it more efficiently, just as you'd have a conversation with a friend or colleague.

For instance, let's say the name of my imposter is Christian. Christian still appears frequently in my life, especially during talks, presentations or important pitches.

My goal here is not to prevent Christian from appearing, but rather to recognise when he does, and separate his thoughts from my own.

By doing this, you can challenge those thoughts, and actually utilise them to good effect. This process should be carried out without self-judgement or pressure. It's similar to how you would respond to a colleague who approaches your desk to ask a question.

Here are some examples of things I've found Christian thinking, and how I now reframe them.

Initial judgemental statement	Reframed statement
Why am I thinking negatively again about this pitch?	I'm starting to think more about this pitch. Thanks for letting me know, Christian.
What if they ask a question I don't know how to answer?	Thanks for the thought. I've got that covered already, Christian.
I can't ask anyone for help. It'll look like I don't know what I'm doing.	By asking someone for support, I can learn from this situation, and how someone else might approach it.

Developing the habit of naming your imposter allows you to leverage it when necessary, while keeping it from defining your entire identity.

Psyche Success Stories —
Amie & Her Imposter Dee

Amie, a New Business Team Lead, found that the self-talk from her imposter was constantly popping up with statements like:

- If this goes wrong, your team is going to think you're unfit to manage.
- Your way is the right way. If you listen to others' suggestions, they'll think you're not confident in what you're doing.
- You should be able to master everything in this role. If you can't, then maybe you shouldn't be a manager.

At first, she was buying into these thoughts, which were being reinforced with confirmation bias.

Once Amie had acknowledged her imposter syndrome, and the two main personas (Perfectionist and Expert), she gave them a collective name: Dee. The name came from a nickname she'd had as a child, when, as she describes it, she was a lot quieter and less experienced in life.

Once she had named her imposter(s), she found every time these thoughts were coming up, she was more conscious of them being driven by Dee. Amie became less judgemental of them, and also found herself validating or challenging those thoughts.

As a result, Amie began to embrace suggestions from her team, was more focused on what she could control in situations, and found her stress levels reduced dramatically as a result.

She now openly talks about Dee with her team, and even with her partner, when Dee shows up in her personal life.

Imagine Your Imposter as the Role of a Villain in a Film

Take a moment to think about one of your favourite action or superhero films. There is always a hero and a villain. Typically, the hero is going about their life, sometimes a little complacently, when the villain enters the scene. Initially, the hero fails when they challenge their adversary.

The hero then embarks on a journey of growth and transformation, eventually returning to defeat the villain in an epic showdown.

It's one of mankind's oldest traditional storylines, from myth and legend. The epic, transformative quest. The heroic odyssey. Challenge, doubt ... and victory.

Think of Batman, who goes to the Lazarus Pit to be rejuvenated and learn new skills before facing the supervillain Bane. This dynamic creates a captivating story and we find ourselves rooting for the hero.

Now, imagine that same movie without the villain. What would be different? First, it probably wouldn't be one of your favourites. There would be no compelling storyline, and most importantly, the hero would remain unchanged. The role of a villain is crucial in making any superhero or action film entertaining.

This is how we can view our imposter – not as the villain, but as the role and change that a villain provokes in a film. Envision yourself as the hero of your own story, with your imposter appearing to test you, forcing you to adapt, learn and grow.

Think back on your greatest achievements in your career and life. Chances are you're most proud of those moments when you confronted a challenge and learnt how to deal with it. Your imposter likely played a part in sparking that growth or change.

Similar to the role of a villain, your imposter helps you identify areas that require improvement or demand more focused time for you to reflect on what you've actually achieved.

Without it, you wouldn't adapt, and you wouldn't experience personal growth. The memories of your successes may not feel as empowering without the presence of your imposter.

Here are some things over my career and life that my imposter, Christian, has been present for and helped me with.

Situation	How my imposter benefited me
Nervous about public speaking	• Got me to focus on my storytelling • Pushed me into more watching and learning from others
Working as a sales coach for a FinTech company	• Allowed me to recognise that my knowledge of the product needed to be better • Got me thinking about how I could build trust and relationships with people I was coaching
Rejected for a role as associate trainer	• Made me recognise that I wanted to work on my skills and expertise • Got me thinking about how I could simplify my content
Thinking I'd be 'found out' before a big sales pitch	• Prompted me to do 2-3 practice runthroughs of the pitch beforehand • Made me think about the questions I might be asked, and how to prepare for them

By reframing your imposter in this way, you adopt a healthier perspective when it rears its head. You start to see it as an impetus to focus on what you can learn or change in order to succeed.

Understanding and reframing your imposter is an important step towards becoming your own biggest champion. Combining this with the tools we walked through earlier can help you develop self-awareness and self-belief, and achieve the success that comes from it.

Your goal is not to completely eliminate your imposter, but rather to acquire the tools necessary to triumph in the face of it.

Once you've accomplished this, your imposter will subside for a while, but accept the possibility that it may resurface when you need it. There will always be another villain to conquer in your story, just like in the best action-adventure films.

The Playbook that you'll find at the end of this guide will point you to other tools that can support you in working on your Imposter Syndrome, and using it to your advantage, if and when you encounter it.

Inspirational Insights

Tom Boston, Brand Growth Manager at MySalesCoach, a sales engagement platform, has a great story to tell related to this. You may have seen Tom's viral videos, which he is becoming known for, pop up on LinkedIn. Something less well known about Tom is that he is a Special Educational Needs and Disabilities (SEND) parent.

He says raising children with additional needs has changed his entire outlook, and helped him understand the importance of celebrating life. Here's his story of becoming his own biggest champion.

"In recent years, I've embarked on a personal odyssey to become my own biggest champion — an endeavour that, interestingly, resonates with many individuals I now guide and mentor," he told me.

"The focal challenge has been contending with Imposter Syndrome, a formidable adversary that complicates the journey of self-affirmation. Reflecting on my initiation into the world of B2B sales in London reveals a narrative rife with feelings of inadequacy.

"The distinctiveness of my appearance, characterised by a bald head, northern roots and a conspicuous ginger beard, fuelled a belief that I was somehow lesser than my counterparts.

"Navigating the transition from a working-class upbringing in Leeds to the corporate landscape of London exacerbated this sense of incongruity. Faced with disparities in economic backgrounds, I concealed aspects of my life to align more closely with my colleagues, contributing to a growing sense of alienation.

"Moreover, my initial foray into sales was fraught with challenges, including a lack of familiarity with industry jargon. Fear of appearing uninformed led me to feign knowledge, even resorting to clandestinely Googling terms like CRM (Customer Relationship Management).

"A pivotal moment in this journey involved realising that my perceived differences were, in fact, my superpower. Contrary to my initial assumptions, not conforming to the stereotypical sales persona turned out to be an asset.

"Openly embracing my authentic self and injecting humour into my professional interactions proved transformative. This shift facilitated my transition from a sales role to a coveted marketing position at Salesloft.

"Today, I leverage humour on social media, host a sales podcast and coach others on building their personal brands. The metamorphosis from doubting my abilities to championing myself has reshaped my entire career trajectory.

"My coaching philosophy centres on instilling confidence in others, urging them to embrace their insecurities and recognise their inherent worth. The choice to champion oneself today becomes the catalyst for future triumphs — an invaluable lesson that my personal journey underscores and one I ardently share with those I mentor."

Activity E8 —
Naming Your Imposter

Take this opportunity to name your imposter, and recognise how they've served you, and continue to do so, in your job.

1. Using the first box below, write down a few names that come to mind. Remember that your imposter name doesn't have to represent a negative figure in your life — it could be an old nickname, an extension of your name, a favourite literary or showbiz character — but make it memorable. Then, circle the one that feels most relevant.
2. In the second box, note down how your imposter supported/benefited you in your life and career.

Ideas for my imposter's name:

How has my imposter supported/benefited me in my life and career?

Your Three Key Takeaways:

1) Recognising and naming your imposter can separate it from your own identity and allow you to respond effectively when it makes an appearance.

2) Your imposter shows up as a signal to get you to pay attention to situations that require change or reframing how you look at them.

3) Imagine your imposter like the role of a villain. Work with it, not against it, to create a memorable story. Your own action-adventure saga.

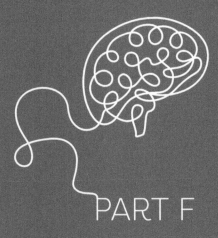

PART F

Sustaining Consistency by Managing & Protecting Your Energy

Imagine your energy as if it were your phone battery, and the different tasks you have each day are like apps. Just like your phone, your personal energy stores have a limited capacity. When you wake up in the morning, you may be running at 35% after a busy weekend, or fully charged from a chilled, stay-at-home weekend. As you go about your day, each task you engage in is like opening and using an app. Some tasks require more energy, just as certain apps drain your phone battery faster.

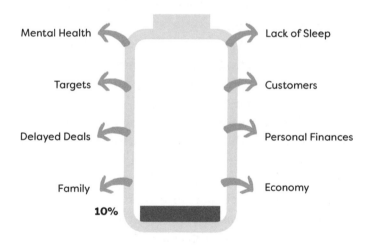

For example, imagine that answering emails is like using a social media app. It may seem harmless at first, but it can quickly drain your energy as you get caught up in reading and responding to numerous messages.

Similarly, attending meetings can be like playing a digital game that uses a lot of processing power. It requires your full attention and can leave you mentally drained.

It's essential to remember that this daily energy management is not just about productivity, but also about well-being. Just like leaving apps running in the background drains your phone battery, unresolved stressors, not setting boundaries, or neglecting to recharge or switch off can gradually drain your physical and mental reserves. Failing to manage or protect your energy properly can lead to a state of burnout.

In this part, I'll provide you with the tools to manage your energy effectively, to ensure that you can create a more consistent and sustainable approach to your sales role and life outside of work.

You'll get a better understanding of the five stages of burnout, the three biggest hidden causes, and the importance that boundaries play in building a sustainable approach.

Additionally, a big part of conserving your energy is becoming more comfortable with saying 'no.' You'll learn why you might find this difficult, and how to become more open to saying it. Let's start by addressing the elephant in the sales room: burnout.

CHAPTER 27

Battling Burnout – Recognising the Five Stages of the Silent Sales Killer

Burnout is a state of chronic physical and emotional exhaustion that often occurs when we're exposed to prolonged stress. This can stem from work-related pressures or personal demands, without the right resources to manage and process them.

It's something to be mindful of in the competitive pressure cooker of sales, where we're constantly chasing targets, dealing with uncontrollable factors and feeling like we're never doing 'enough.'

But burnout doesn't just sneak up on you overnight. There are signs you can look out for, in yourself and in others, that can help you prevent it.

Let's start with some of the most common signs and symptoms of burnout, and the five stages, initially described by psychologist Herbert Freudenberger and further examined by social psychologist and academic Christina Maslach.[24]

The Five Stages of Burnout:
1. The Honeymoon Phase
2. The Balancing Act (Stress Onset)
3. Chronic Stress
4. The Crisis Stage (Burnout)
5. Habitual Burnout

#1 The Honeymoon Phase

What is it?

The first stage of burnout, known as the Honeymoon Phase, is like the calm before the storm. That can particularly be the case for us in sales roles. It's a time when we're often blissfully unaware that something might be amiss. We might sense a subtle unease in our gut, but we tend to dismiss it as regular stress or 'just part of the job.'

At the outset, we're typically brimming with energy and optimism, fully committed to proving ourselves and excelling in new situations.

This is where the idea of the Honeymoon Phase kicks in. It's the period when we start developing coping mechanisms that help us handle the challenges and pressures, effectively masking the burnout that's looming on the horizon.

When is it likely to occur?

Here are some situations where you might find it showing up:
- Starting a new job
- Getting promoted and beginning the unfamiliar new role

- Taking on new responsibilities at work, such as overseeing the team when your manager is away, doing internal training or contributing to the sales playbook
- Kicking off the new financial or calendar year
- Working through ambitious new product launches
- Being part of an exciting vision or culture, where we disregard this feeling because of the other positives we're receiving

What are the signs?
Here are some things you're likely to encounter during this initial phase:
- Being in a constant state of alertness
- Feeling the need to prove yourself every day, as if it will be a complete failure if you don't
- Saying 'yes' to every request, without reflecting on how you're currently spending your time and energy
- Continually neglecting and sacrificing your personal time outside of work
- Having increased energy, as if you're experiencing an adrenaline rush

This stage is one that most salespeople will find themselves in, and there isn't anything inherently wrong with the excitement . But like most things in this book, it's all about how you respond to it.

If you don't address it or ignore it, you'll find yourself moving to stage two. However, if you work on applying the tools we cover here, you can utilise this stage and prevent burnout from creeping up on you.

#2 The Balancing Act
(Stress Onset)

What is it?

The second stage of burnout, sometimes called The Balancing Act or Stress Onset, is where things start to get more noticeable. It's when you begin to realise that some days are tougher than others.

As time goes on, the combined weight of these challenges starts to wear on your emotional and physical health, and the effects become more evident. During this period, wrangling your emotions can become quite the juggling act, making it harder to maintain the composure and optimism needed in sales.

When is it likely to occur?

Here are some situations where you might find it most likely showing up:

- Near the end of the quarter or in a year-end push
- When market or economy shifts unexpectedly
- A sudden spike in workload, perhaps from covering a colleague on leave or who has been laid off, or taking on additional customers

What are the signs?

Here are some indications that you're into this stage:

- You become more irritable, frustrated or even tearful on the days when you're noticing stress building up
- Despite your efforts, you may feel like your work doesn't meet your own standards or the expectations of others

- On these tough days, you might struggle to stay focused, feel fatigued and find it hard to stay awake, and become overly anxious about unfinished tasks
- You have a diminishing sense of satisfaction and accomplishment from what you're doing

#3 Chronic Stress

What is it?

When prolonged stress remains unresolved, it can bring us to the third stage of burnout, known as Chronic Stress. It can feel like a relentless, crushing weight on your shoulders. Chronic stress isn't picky – it affects both your mental and physical wellbeing, intensifying the emotions you're wrestling with from the earlier stages.

In sales, where self-regulation and emotional intelligence are crucial, this can be particularly challenging. And be aware that chronic stress doesn't clock out when you leave the office. It follows you home, affecting your personal life, your passions and your overall sense of wellbeing, leaving you fighting to regain your equilibrium.

When is it likely to occur?

Here are some situations where you might find this persistent stress most likely showing up:

- Consistent, demanding pressure from above to hit targets, without coaching or support
- Continuing to neglect your personal wellbeing, avoiding taking time off, and even if you do, finding yourself working (or feeling that you should be) while on holiday
- When prolonged stress isn't spotted or addressed by the salesperson, manager or company

- Inconsistent performance, with the rollercoaster ride of hitting your target, but then struggling the next month or quarter, without investigating why

What are the signs?

Here are some signs of struggling with the Chronic Stress stage:

- Being overwhelmed by feelings of sadness, resentment, or even exhibiting aggressive behaviour as a result of our inability to cope effectively
- Sleep disturbances, changes in appetite, and frequent low-grade illness due to a weakened immune system
- Simple tasks that were once manageable now feel overwhelming, leading to a sense of powerlessness and diminished self-worth
- Mounting pressure to meet daily obligations becomes increasingly challenging, to the point where we may resort to the crutch of alcohol or drug abuse
- Finding it harder to get enjoyment from activities that once brought us pleasure

#4 The Crisis Stage (Burnout)

What is it?
In the fourth phase, known as the Crisis Stage or simply 'Burnout,' everything peaks. For salespeople, it's like hitting rock bottom. What used to be occasional or manageable symptoms now consume our daily lives, and we start seeing the terribleness as normal.

In the Crisis Stage, these symptoms become deeply ingrained patterns that hinder our ability to function, making everyday work challenging.

When is it likely to occur?
Here are some situations where this is most likely to manifest itself:

- External outputs of chronic stress (working longer hours, looking like a 'hard worker,' pushing continuously) are celebrated and normalised as part of the business culture, without digging beneath the surface of the impact on the salesperson
- Decrease in sales performance, from what used to be a more consistent level, with the salesperson expending too much energy on uncontrollables, allowing limiting beliefs and thinking that more hours worked equals increased performance, without any real rational approach
- Staying in a chronic state of stress for too long, and not taking a break, with symptoms like fatigue, insomnia, headaches and irritability having an ongoing negative impact on work, health and wellbeing

What are the signs?

Here are some indications that a person is deep into this stage:

- Our physical health may deteriorate due to prolonged exposure to stress hormones, a weakened immune system and disrupted sleep patterns
- Our mental health can be significantly impacted, leading to an increased vulnerability to anxiety disorders, depression and other psychological issues
- Our relationships may suffer as emotional exhaustion and detachment strain our connections with loved ones
- Any sense of fulfilment and accomplishment in our work and personal lives erodes, leaving us feeling dissatisfied and adrift
- Becoming disengaged and indifferent to feedback

#5 Habitual Burnout

What is it?

In the fifth and final stage, Habitual Burnout, these toxic symptoms have become entrenched in every aspect of our lives. Despite our attempts to recover, we're stuck in a cycle of chronic exhaustion, emotional depletion and deteriorating wellbeing.

This phase takes a toll on physical and mental health, further weakening the immune system and exacerbating anxiety, depression and burnout-related malaise. Coping becomes increasingly challenging, with the mounting pain and anguish often requiring professional help.

When is it likely to occur?

Here are some situations where you might find this deepest, darkest phase showing up:

- When the crisis stage of burnout isn't dealt with by the salesperson or the company — no break is taken, management doesn't spot it, etc.
- If work-related stressors, such as unrealistic high quotas or workplace culture issues, persist without relief or intervention
- When you have not developed effective coping strategies or haven't sought help and support to manage stress
- Consistently failing to prioritise self-care, at work and outside of it, leaving you particularly vulnerable

What are the signs?

Along with the signs and symptoms of the previous stage, you can also see the following:

- Feeling persistent, deep-seated exhaustion that doesn't improve with rest or sleep. You may wake up tired and struggle to find the energy to get through the day
- Numbness or detachment, leaving you emotionally drained and unable to connect with your feelings or those of others
- Cynicism and apathy towards work and life in general, making you highly critical of your job and pretty much everything else, with a 'nothing really matters' or 'what's the point' attitude

Recognising and addressing habitual burnout is a complex process, best addressed by seeking medical assistance, therapy and support networks. If you or someone you know is nearing or in the throes of burnout, talking openly about it and seeking help is imperative. You won't be seen as a burden or weak for talking about feeling this way. It's also important to recognise that, even though you might feel there are so many people worse off in the world right now, you are still entitled to feel the way you do and have your own challenges. Don't suffer in silence.

Overcoming habitual burnout is a demanding journey, but with the appropriate awareness, attention and support, people can regain control over their lives, restore their physical and mental health, and move towards a more balanced and satisfying future.

Inspirational Insights

Pete Crosby, Cofounder and CEO of management consultancy Revelesco, is one of those people you always feel fortunate to speak to and hear on panels. He has a vast amount of experience, and the way he shares his insights and stories always captures an audience's attention.

Pete is also a father, and was told when his first daughter was born that she wouldn't live past five years old. She defied the odds and is now 23, but this shaped Pete in his career, in terms of prioritising family. In putting them first, he's said 'no' to plenty of things and stepped away from exciting opportunities.

But it wasn't always like that. A real turning point came in 2019, when he was working for marketing platform Ometria and in the middle of a boardroom presentation. His phone went off and he was told his daughter had suffered a suspected heart attack, and there was a helicopter on the way.

Fortunately, it wasn't a heart attack, but he realised he'd had enough of travelling home for emergencies from places around the world.

He took the self-administered Oldenburg Burnout Inventory test and immediately recognised that he was exhausted. Looking back now, the signs were evident, but at the time he didn't reflect on them. For instance, he was travelling extensively, with 40 trips to China in a single year.

When he was home, he wasn't really present, often catching up on sleep and not being the husband or father he wanted to be. So, Pete stepped away from that bruising environment and since then has focused on being more intentional with how he takes care of himself.

Pete has said you should look at your sales career and mindset like a professional athlete. If you want to be able to perform in a match, you want to think about what contributes to making a go of it. And not just for a one-off match, but a whole season — that important sustainability factor. Without this, you go looking for all the ways to win in the short term, which is a fast-track to burnout.

This encompasses the sleep you get, what you eat and how you're training your brain to deal with the all doubts and knockbacks along the way.

Don't just think about the tangible things like calls made or what you say in a meeting, but all the component parts that help you perform at your best and get you into a healthy headspace.

Pete's topline advice: If you want elite performance, you need a world-class athlete's approach to the way you think and take care of yourself.

Activity F1 —
Reflection on Burnout

Take some time now to reflect on where you feel you might be, or have been, along the five-stage burnout spectrum.

Awareness is the first and most important step to working on proactively preventing burnout, or addressing it if you're experiencing it already.

Your Three Key Takeaways:

1) Think of your energy as your phone battery, and be conscious of what could be using it up on an hourly, daily
   and weekly basis.

2) Burnout doesn't occur overnight. Be conscious of the five
   stages — their breeding-ground situations, symptoms
   and implications.

3) Awareness of where you or others might be along the
   spectrum is the first and most important step to preventing or addressing burnout.

CHAPTER 28

The Three Biggest Hidden Causes of Burnout

You're probably aware of some of the obvious causes of burnout in sales, such as the pressure of constant targets or sky-high expectations, but I want to focus on three of the primary hidden contributors and how they're often overlooked.

Recognising these, and knowing how to manage them, can go a long way to proactively preventing burnout and creating a consistent, sustainable approach in your sales position.

#1 Neglecting Your Non-Work Identities

One of the top hidden culprits is neglecting our non-work identities. These identities, such as being a sibling, parent, volunteer, coach, partner, make us who we are.

They've played a crucial role in shaping us into the person we are today, and are extremely valuable in our lives. Unfortunately, these identities often become the first things we start to neglect when everything doesn't go according to plan in our career.

It's easy to get caught up in any target-driven job and focus solely on hitting those numbers. Over time, we might even start to measure our self-worth solely based on those results.

When we centre our entire identity in our work, it's easy to become overly critical and judgemental of ourselves when we're not performing well. This constant pressure to put more and more into our job leads to increased stress, and eventually full-scale burnout.

To avoid this, it's important to become more mindful of your non-work identities, and how you protect time and energy for them. Another factor to help with this is becoming more aware of the value you bring to your non-work identities.

Here's an example of this from a salesperson, Zena, who I worked with recently when she realised she was neglecting her non-work identities.

Your non-work identity	How do I bring value to this identity?	What does success look like for this identity?
Sister	• Spending quality time with her sibling • Emotional support when she's having a tough day	Being the person she goes to when she's struggling, and always knowing they'll be there for each other, even if not in person
Auntie	• Being a role model • Teaching her niece valuable life lessons	Her niece looking up to her, and looking forward to regularly spending time with her
Girlfriend	• Supporting her partner and inspiring one another • Words of affirmation • Dealing with difficult life challenges	Boyfriend feeling supported, inspired and happy within their relationship. Always feels like he can be open and honest with her, and that it's not burdening her
Runner	• Taking care of her physical, emotional and mental health through exercise • Giving herself a sense of accomplishment with each run	Going for 2-3 runs a week and listening to a podcast during each one, which together make it special 'me time'

Inspirational Insights

Ollie Sharpe, Chief Commercial Officer at revenue management platform Lative, has long been an advocate of
embracing non-work identities. I first met Ollie when he
was working at Salesloft, and he's been a real champion of
taking care of your mental and general wellbeing in sales.

Previously, while working at LinkedIn, Ollie learnt that his
wife had cancer, and his boss immediately advised him
to prioritise her. It stuck with him, and he recognised that
although he still cared about work, it was a vessel for the
other things in his life.

Ollie has gone on to share this with many others. I've spoken with numerous salespeople on his teams, and they all
say that he got to know their non-work identities — who
they really are as people — and has always emphasised
their importance.

The key here isn't saying you shouldn't care about your
work, or care less. It's about reminding yourself why you're
doing what you're doing, and staying conscious of what
else is important and a priority in your life.

These non-work identities are your fuel; make sure you're
investing in them. Find a place where leaders will value
these fundamental human aspects of you, rather than seeing them as distractions.

Activity F2 — Acknowledging Your Non-Work Identities

Now it's your turn to create your own version of all this, to become more conscious of your non-work identities and their value. Use the table below to answer the following questions:

1. In the first column, write down two of your primary non-work identities.
2. In the second column, note how you bring value to these identities.
3. In the final column, indicate what success looks like for that identity, however you might define that.

My non-work identity	How do I bring value to this identity?	What does success look like for this identity?

This exercise allows us to gain a broader perspective and recognise the intangible ways in which we make an impact in our lives beyond work.

Being conscious of our non-work identities also helps us create motivation and goals, because they're likely connected to the reasons we chose a career in sales and why we strive for success in those endeavors.

Keeping them top-of-mind helps us maintain perspective, drives our purpose forward, and serves as a constant reminder that our sales quota does not define our self-worth.

#2 Unsustainable Drive

Let me be clear: I'm not saying you shouldn't be driven. That would be absurd. Instead, the crucial point here is to consider the unsustainable aspects that come from this feeling.

Picture this: You've just finished a workout at the gym, a run, a hike, or any sport. You're on an endorphin high, feeling incredibly motivated, thoroughly pumped, positive feelings rushing through you.

But no matter how great you feel in that moment, if you were to attempt the same gruelling workout or run again, your body would would eventually reach its limits, and it would fail on you. You'd feel absolutely wrecked.

This perspective also applies to sales, and how we handle our drive. It's easy to have a fantastic week, month or quarter and think, 'Let's just do that all over again!'

However, before diving back in headfirst, it's important to ask yourself whether this exact approach is sustainable. Can you realistically keep up this pace without it negatively affecting you, at work and in other areas of your life?

Let's say you worked practically every weekend to smash your quarterly target. You never left the office before 7:30 pm on weekdays, and frequently cancelled plans with friends to focus on work.

Let me tell you, that's not a viable approach in the long run. This kind of mindset neglects our non-work identities and can create limiting beliefs, making us think the only way to succeed is by following those extreme behaviours.

Instead, take the time to evaluate whether your behaviours and actions are realistically sustainable. Sure, in sales we sometimes burn the midnight oil or work on weekends, but that shouldn't be the norm. It can't be the constant.

One comment I've been hearing more on this is, 'But if it feels good, why shouldn't I put in the after-hours work?' I'm not saying that you shouldn't under any circumstances work late, but that it should not become a manic compulsion.

Eating junk food, staying out all night drinking or inviting the in-laws for Christmas may feel good in the moment, but can be things you look back on with regret.

This idea of it feeling good here and now often neglects the long view, ignoring all the nasty implications.

Activity F3 —
Are You Working Sustainably?

Answer the questions below to establish whether your behaviour is sustainable, and if not, how to address that.

Question	Your Answer
1. What am I currently doing in my job that could negatively impact me in the long run (not taking leave, working weekends, leaving office at 9 pm, etc.)?	
2. Would I want these behaviours to become the norm for me in my career?	
3. What's the potential impact of not addressing these in the long run (losing friends, feeling more stressed, becoming unfit, breaking up with my partner)?	
4. What are one or two things I can do to make this more sustainable?	

This kind of self-reflection and mindfulness will help you develop healthy, sustainable habits that still allow you to achieve success without experiencing burnout from constantly sprinting and coming to a sudden stop.

We'll delve into tools and suggestions for dealing with this in the coming chapters.

#3 Lack of Self-Reflection

We can get so caught up in the hustle and bustle of our daily lives that we forget to hit the pause button and reflect on how we're really doing. It's like we're on autopilot, constantly pushing forward without taking the time to check in with ourselves.

Be aware that a lack of self-reflection can quietly sneak up on us and become a hidden cause of burnout.

When we don't pause to understand our needs, boundaries and emotions, we end up running on empty, pushing ourselves to the limit without even realising.

It's like driving a car without stopping to refuel or make sure the engine's running smoothly. (More on this analogy later.)

Taking a moment to reflect, to really tune in to our thoughts and feelings, can help us identify early signs of burnout and make necessary adjustments.

It's like giving ourselves permission to recharge and find a better balance, so we can avoid that exhaustion and overwhelm down the road.

Psyche Success Stories –
Liam & The Power of Reflection

Liam, a Mid-Market Account Executive, grappled with the challenge of inconsistency in his sales performance. Richocheting between quarters where he overachieved and subsequent slow periods, he found himself stuck in a repetitive cycle of burnout.

This pattern created instability in his overall results and took a toll on Liam's wellbeing and relationships outside of work.

Recognising the need for a change, he began working with me. Acknowledging the negative impact on both professional and personal aspects of his life, Liam made a conscious decision to adopt a more mindful approach.

He committed to cultivating habits that would ensure success without succumbing to the burnout cycle. Among other things, this involved reframing the challenges into questions like, 'How can I plan my week to avoid working weekends?'

Instead of replicating intense behaviours from successful quarters, he embraced a more mindful, sustainable approach to his daily routine, leading to more consistent performance.

This included time-blocking his week to become more efficient, and ensuring that he was investing time and energy in his non-work identities, to give him a more well-rounded sense of achievement and fulfilment.

This shift not only improved Liam's overall wellbeing but contributed to a more stable, consistently strong performance on the job, which then led to a promotion a few months later.

Your Three Key Takeaways:

1) Make sure you're investing time and energy in your non-work identities, and recognise their value.

2) Think about creating more sustainable approaches to your career and outside life. Sometimes the things that feel good in the moment aren't sustainable in the long run.

3) Give yourself space to self-reflect on how you've progressed and what you've achieved. Without it, you'll feel like you're constantly chasing and never winning.

CHAPTER 29

Managing Your Energy – Setting Effective Boundaries

Imagine you had £86,400 in your bank account, and someone stole £15 from it. Would you spend the rest of the money trying to get it back? Probably not.

Well, there are 86,400 seconds in a day, and we often have moments where people steal 15, 30 or 60 seconds from us. What sometimes happens is that we end up wasting the rest of our day dwelling on those insignificant moments, like a deal that got postponed or a call that didn't go as planned.

We end up creating more stress for ourselves, turning a stressful moment into a stressful day.

They say time is money in sales, but more importantly, time is energy, and energy is your most valuable currency. It determines your success in managing a high-performance mindset. It's also key to how you take care of your mental wellbeing and prevent burnout.

Take a look at how you've invested your energy today. Are you putting it into things that will give you a return, either immediately or in the long run? Or, are you wasting it by dwelling on things you can't change, which only leads to frustration and negative self-judgement?

Where you invest your energy and how you protect it is tremendously important. In this part we'll explore ways to become more conscious of how you're managing and protecting your precious stores of personal energy.

One way of doing this while making sure you're not neglecting your non-work identities, which we touched on earlier, is by defining your non-negotiables.

Defining Your Non-Negotiables

This is a fundamental aspect of managing your energy effectively. By identifying essential activities you want to accomplish each week or month, you can optimise your time management, prioritizing the things that contribute to your productivity, wellbeing and success.

Moreover, in setting these non-negotiables, you'll see to it that you don't neglect activities that bring you ful-filment or joy, aiding in the prevention of burnout and fostering a healthy mind.

An added benefit is consistency in completing tasks, eliminating the need to constantly reassess priorities. This keeps you on track towards your goals and helps reduce stress and decision fatigue. The non-negotiables serve as anchors, grounding you in your values, career, goals and self-care.

Here are some examples of essential non-negotiables from salespeople I've worked with:

- Date night with partner 1-2 times a week
- Pickleball with friends every Wednesday evening
- Being home to read kids a bedtime story at least 3 times a week

- Going to guitar lesson every Saturday morning
- Making x number of prospecting calls or customer touchpoints a day
- Learning one new thing each week that contributes to industry knowledge or personal development
- Yoga every Wednesday morning before work
- Keeping phone away from the table at meal times

Daily and weekly non-negotiables provide a sense of consistency and stability amidst the ebb and flow of sales and life. They become reliably controllable touchstones that you can focus on, which stops you from getting overly wrapped up in the outcome or neglecting what's otherwise important to you.

In summary, daily and weekly non-negotiables are not mere routines or tasks. They're the building blocks of a fulfilling and balanced approach to your profession and your personal life. They remind you to invest in yourself and prioritise what you can control, and what truly matters.

Inspirational Insights

We heard earlier in the book from Ursula Llabres, Director of Customer Growth at Meta's Reality Labs. Here's her take on the importance of non-negotiables:

"I consider exercise a non-negotiable, essential part of my life," she told me. "I've learnt that any form of physical activity, particularly outdoor running, is essential for my mental wellbeing. It's my way of ensuring I stay calm and collected rather than turning into a less pleasant version of myself.

"I fit exercise into my schedule wherever possible, whether it's early mornings, during lunch or right after work. It's a non-negotiable commitment. I also take time to prepare healthy meals. I invest a lot of effort in this on the weekends because I enjoy cooking.

"Maintaining a healthy lifestyle, which includes regular exercise, good nutrition, sleep management and stress reduction, can be challenging. It's not always easy, and motivation can waver, but the rewards are indisputable.

"Steadfastness and persistence are vital because excuses can be tempting. However, by persisting, you directly influence your ability to succeed and find joy in life."

Before we get into activities that can help keep the non-negotiables in focus, be mindful of not trying to overload yourself with too many to start off with. You may come away with plenty of ideas on this, which is great. But start small and get them implemented, rather than attempting 5-10 at once and then abandoning it all after a few weeks.

Activity F4 —
Defining Your Non-Negotiables

Take some time to think about some non-negotiables that you already have hard-wired in place, or could implement in your daily/weekly life.

1. Using the first box below, scribble down any rough ideas of what those non-negotiables could be. This is just an ideas box, so note anything that comes to mind.
2. Under that, using the left-hand column, identify 1-2 non-negotiables from the list that you'd like to start with.
3. In the right-hand column, write down when you intend to take action and implement these. Remember, without a specific time, day and/or location, they won't stick.

Non-negotiables ideas:	
Your initial 1-2 Non-Negotiables	**When you intend to act on them (morning/lunch time/evening, at a specific time)**
1.	
2.	

Knowing Your Upper & Lower Boundaries

It's not just defining your non-negotiables each day that helps you effectively manage your energy. It's also becoming more conscious of giving yourself a benchmark to maintain and work towards. It's setting and remaining conscious of your upper and lower boundaries.

Imagine your typical to-do list, with perhaps 30+ tasks each day. And that's probably lowballing that number for some of you. How many times have you felt like you're endlessly busy but not making any real progress? Maybe you've had those days where you only complete half of your list and feel like you're falling short, or you stay late trying to make a dent.

Then there are those moments when you start questioning whether you are doing enough in your role, because you're only fixated on your number (the outcome) and not aware of the progress being made by your input. This can lead to negative thinking, increased stress, lack of self-recognition and a constant strain on your energy levels.

All of these challenges often come down to not defining what 'enough' looks like. It's like going for a run without setting a time or distance. You'll always come away feeling disappointed, because you didn't give yourself a benchmark for success.

Even when you do sometimes set the bar for what you want to achieve in a day, it's an all-or-nothing target, such as, 'I have to get everything on this to-do list done, and if I don't my day will have been a failure.' Or, your list is overly outcome-focused. For example:

- Close three deals before Friday
- Book four meetings today
- Play tennis three evenings this week

The problem with having a list of purely outcome-focused goals is that they aren't as controllable. It's important to focus on the controllable inputs you can pursue that sequentially lead to these accomplishments.

To handle both of these challenges, it's more effective to set a range to work towards, known as Upper and Lower Boundaries.

Your lower threshold represents the bare minimum you want to achieve each day or week, while your upper boundary is a stretch target.

Lower boundaries give you a sense of satisfaction even on challenging days, when everything seems to go wrong. They remind you that despite setbacks, you still accomplished something.

On the other hand, upper boundaries prevent you from overcommitting to one thing and neglecting everything else. It's like overworking a specific body part at the gym and not being able to use it properly for days afterward.

We often gravitate towards certain tasks, while neglecting others that are also important.

Overleaf are some of the types of upper and lower boundaries you could start introducing into your day, week or month.

Task/ Activity	Frequency	Lower Boundary	Upper Boundary
Cold calls	Daily	30 per day	50 per day
Email follow-ups	Daily	25 per day	35 per day
LinkedIn outreach	Daily	15 new prospects per day	20 new prospects per day
Exercise	Weekly	A walk before work or at lunch time each day	Three gym visits
Product/ industry knowledge	Weekly/ Monthly	Read one industry blog	Read one industry blog and attend one sales-relevant webinar a month
Non-work identity activities	Monthly	Two date nights One game of tennis with a friend	Five date nights Two games of tennis with a friend

As you can see from these examples, it's also valuable to incorporate your non-work identities into your boundary-setting. As we've discussed, that plays a crucial role in managing and protecting your energy and your mental wellbeing.

You may wonder when the best time is to set these boundaries, and how often to revisit that prioritisation. How often is a matter of personal preference, but I'd suggest experimenting. This checkpoint can be done daily, but most sales people I work with prefer weekly. The best time to focus on them is on a Friday afternoon, the week before you intend to pursue those activities.

This way, you can enter the weekend feeling prepared, and avoid the 'Sunday scaries' or going into Monday morning unprepared.

Also, when priortising for the week ahead, make sure to reflect on the week just ended, and what you've noticed and achieved through setting these lower and upper boundaries.

Incorporating this with the self-reflection Activity E3 – assessing your weekly/monthly wins – can support you in building momentum, self-awareness and self-recognition for your efforts and the energy you invest.

Psyche Success Stories – Christina & Defining 'Enough'

Meet Christina, an SDR struggling with that constant feeling of never doing enough. Often finding herself spending too much time on one activity while neglecting others, Christina grappled with a lack of defined benchmarks for success in her daily tasks. This led to constantly beating herself up over her activity and progress.

After we started to work together, she began implementing upper and lower boundaries into her daily and weekly schedule. These included:

Activity	Frequency	Lower Boundary	Upper Boundary
Cold calls	Daily	40 per day	60 per day
Self-Development	Weekly	Listen to one podcast this week	Take in a podcast and a LinkedIn course this week
Exercise	Daily/Weekly	A walk at lunch time each day	Two gym visits, with a walk to and from there
Networking	Monthly	Have a coffee with two colleagues and ask sales-related questions	Attend two external networking events this month

Christina started to recognise that the lower boundaries provided a sense of accomplishment on challenging days, serving as a reminder that progress was being made, even in the face of setbacks.

Meanwhile, the upper boundaries prevented her from over-committing to one task and neglecting others, fostering a more balanced, holistic approach to her daily activities.

Having direction gave her a greater sense of focus and something clear and concise to work towards. This meant she could plan her time more effectively, with an eye on reaching specific goals.

This strategic shift not only alleviated the pressure of an all-or-nothing mindset, but also allowed Christina to focus on controllable inputs rather than fixating on outcome-focused goals.

By incorporating upper and lower boundaries into her daily routine, Christina achieved a healthier balance in task prioritisation, and experienced a more sustainable and fulfilling approach to her role as an SDR.

Activity F5 —
Defining Your Upper
& Lower Boundaries

Now it's time for you to think about what your potential upper and lower boundaries could look like, and their frequency. Fill in the table below, using the previous examples as inspiration. Try to take action and implement these. Remember, without a specific time, day and/or location, they won't stick.

Task/ Activity	Frequency (Daily/ Weekly)	Lower Boundary	Upper Boundary

And now, make it real. Establish and stick to lower (routine) and upper (stretch) boundaries for both the work and personal aspects of your life.

Your Three Key Takeaways:

1) Master your time: Treat seconds like currency. Don't waste energy on insignificant moments. Time is vital, in a sales career and for managing your mind.

2) Set boundaries for success: define realistic lower and upper boundaries for daily tasks. They'll help you benchmark success and spend your time wisely.

3) Be conscious of your energy: invest in controllable inputs, not just outcomes.

CHAPTER 30

The Power of Saying 'No'

There are so many times each day where you get asked a question on Slack, asked in the office 'if you have five minutes,' see an unexpected meeting show up in your calendar, or are asked by friends if you can make it for a drink after work (which will certainly end up being more than one).

All of these moments can feel difficult to push back on. Let's start by exploring why we can find it hard to say no.

Social psychologist Dr. Vanessa K. Bohns highlighted the discomfort people feel when refusing tasks or favours in her research review on influence. She found that we often agree to things we don't really want to do because we do not want to be seen as difficult or disappointing to others.[25]

In the workplace, declining a task or not immediately answering a question, can be perceived as a sign that we lack commitment or competence, especially in healthy and growing company cultures where being a team player is valued.

Another reason we struggle to say no can be our genuine desire to help others. Assisting those in need gives us a sense of purpose and satisfaction. However, in our altruistic eagerness to help, we often neglect our own wellbeing and limitations.

We forget that constantly saying yes, without balance, can lead to burnout and resentment. Our concern for our reputation and a compulsion to prove ourselves can override the importance of prioritising our own needs and boundaries.

It's worth noting that our responses to others' requests shape their expectations and behaviours towards us. For example, if we always respond immediately on Slack, others will assume it's the norm and come to rely on us for quick answers.

This pattern becomes ingrained in their minds and creates even more pressure over time. Our primal brain is always looking for the quickest way to achieve something, so in this case, that person's mind could start thinking, 'I know Chris will always have an answer for me, so I don't need to spend time trying to find it myself.'

Understand that saying no is not inherently negative or selfish. It's an essential part of self-care, setting boundaries and maintaining a healthy balance in our relationships and responsibilities.

Learning to say no respectfully and assertively empowers us to prioritise our wellbeing while fostering open communication and mutual understanding with others.

We, of course, need to be conscious of the difference between what we can reasonably say no to or push back on, and what is actually part of our role and important to manage.

So, how can you work on this and become more effective at saying no? Here are some practical ways to do so.

Nine Ways to Improve Your Ability to Say 'No'

1. **Keep your goals and reasons in mind.** Before turning down a request, remind yourself why you're making that decision. Knowing your priorities, limitations and goals will help you express your refusal with clarity and confidence. Reminding yourself what you've already said yes to, and may need to stop accepting, can help with the problem of over-committing.

2. **Ask for context.** If someone in the team is asking for 'five minutes' or help with 'a quick question,' you are entitled to ask them for more context before stopping what you're doing. Ask if it's really going to require just five minutes, precisely what is it they want to know and, when relevant, if they've looked to find the answer themselves before coming to you.

3. **Establish urgency.** We're great at establishing urgency with prospects and customers, but often forget to apply the same logic in-house. If someone is coming to you with a question or a request for your time, look to establish the degree of urgency. Ask questions like, 'What's the impact going to be of this not getting done this morning?' to help gauge the necessity. If it's not all that pressing, refer to the point below.

4. **Saying 'Not right now.'** You don't always have to reject a request outright. Offering an alternative, like 'Not right now, but how about after 2pm?' can be a constructive compromise. Suggest a specific time when you can provide support, giving the person a chance to explore other options or seek help elsewhere.

You can proactively do this with those who may come to you regularly. For instance, it's easy enough to say that you'll be on customer calls for most of the day, but anytime between 2-4 pm would work if it isn't a burning issue.

5. **Be transparent about your workload.** When faced with additional tasks, openly communicate about your current commitments. Especially when approached by a manager, share the nature of your workload and ask for guidance on prioritization, or potential offloading of lower-priority tasks to accommodate the new request.

6. **Understand task duration.** Developing a sense of how long different activities take can help you better manage your time. Consider using methodologies like the Pomodoro Technique, which involves focused work blocks, to gain awareness of the time required for your role. This understanding will help you make informed decisions about taking on additional tasks.

7. **Block non-meeting time in your calendar.** Proactively use your calendar to schedule dedicated blocks of time for important activities. Plan ahead to protect these slots from meetings or other obligations. Also, remember to allocate breaks to avoid feeling overwhelmed and having to decline due to a packed schedule. When necessary, activating a Do Not Disturb notification on messaging services can help reduce anxiety over how a non-response will be perceived.

8. **Communicate your efforts to improve.** Let others know that you're actively working on avoiding over-commitment and its impact on your job performance and wellbeing. Sharing your intentions and struggles fosters understanding and support from those around you, reducing the likelihood of being continually bombarded with requests.

9. **Remind yourself of when you said 'yes' too many times.** Think back to how you felt when you said you'd work on your day off, got involved in an email thread that had nothing to do with you, or sat on a meandering, unproductive call with someone. Those are stressful, frustrating situations. Reminding yourself of the feeling you had when you didn't say no, when you could have, gives you a stronger impetus to decline when faced with these kinds of distractions.

Remember, saying no is a valuable skill that allows you to prioritise your needs, maintain work-life balance and establish boundaries. With practice and awareness, you can become more confident and effective in respectfully declining requests.

Here are some examples of how you could apply the tips above when it makes sense to say no.

Improving how you say no	How and when can you implement this?
Establish urgency and context.	Every time a colleague asks for some time, I will first ask for context and gauge how urgent it is.
Block non-meeting time in your calendar.	When planning for the following week on Friday afternoons, I will do this calendar housekeeping in advance.
'Not right now.'	I'll proactively tell colleagues what my window of free time will be for any non-urgent questions.

Inspirational Insights

Alfie Marsh, Cofounder & CEO at Toolflow.ai, a provider of artificial intelligence tools, is a firm believer in the well-placed 'no.'

"Saying no to things that drain your energy is an act of self-care," he told me. "It allows you to say yes to what truly matters to you and preserves your wellbeing."

Alfie, who I initially met through Ollie Sharpe, who we featured elsewhere in this guide, came on my podcast a few years back and shares valuable insights via LinkedIn and his newsletter.

He champions the mindset shift to saying no when it makes sense, while reminding yourself of your priorities and the benefits that focus will deliver.

Activity F6 —
Working on Saying 'No'

Saying you need to get better at saying no isn't enough. Take a moment to reflect on the tips, as well as the examples above, and note down which 2-3 of these you could start utilizing, and how you'd go about doing so.

Improving how you say no	How and when can you implement this?

Your Three Key Takeaways:

1) Saying no isn't always selfish; it's self-care. Prioritise what matters.

2) Recognising why saying no can feel hard allows you to challenge and constructively address that thinking.

3) Keep your goals in mind, establish whether requests from others are truly urgent, and communicate to improve your comfort with saying no.

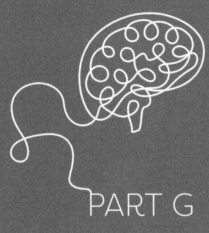

Finding Your Off Switch to Recharge in Sales

You can have the most efficient means of managing and protecting your energy in sales, but if you're not implementing ways to recharge that energy, burnout will eventually catch up with you and consume you.

The nature of sales and how we sometimes approach life means we can often be quite reactive with this, but there are ways to become more effectively proactive with it.

This final part of the guide will support you in becoming more mindful of the ways – proactively and reactively – you can recharge throughout your day and week.

It covers why we can find it so difficult to switch off, and offers tactics you can use to improve on this in the short term, helping to preserve your evenings and weekends. We'll also provide advice on implementing pit stops, for longer breaks throughout your year.

You'll finish this part of the guide with an array of tools to support you in building healthy habits to recharge your energy. This will help you build a more sustainable approach to your sales career that doesn't jeopardise your mental wellbeing along the way, but instead nurtures and strengthens it.

CHAPTER 31

Why Switching Off in Sales Feels So Hard

It's important to find time and space to switch off, whether that be a quiet evening, weekend or heading off for a couple of weeks on holiday.

Yet, the fast pace and constant drive for progress in sales can make it challenging for us to do so.

Whether it's thinking about creating a cadence, preparing for an upcoming demo, constantly checking email near the end of the quarter, or even pondering why we can't stop waving at the end of Zoom calls, there's the imperative to always be up and running.

This difficulty with disconnecting can interfere with our sleep, impact our ability to be present with friends and family, and contribute to an accumulation of stress. If not effectively managed, this can lead to constant anxiety and burnout.

So, if we know that taking time off is so beneficial, why don't we do it? Here are some reasons why you may be finding it difficult to take that all-important down time.

1. We're so busy in our day, we don't have time or space to reflect on it

Imagine being an actor or actress in a CGI film. You're on set every day, filming in front of green screens and people in digitally-wired suits. None of it makes sense at the time, until you eventually watch the finished movie, in all its computer generated, special effects glory. In a way, that's very similar to our day-to-day experience in sales.

We're so immersed in it that we often don't have time to reflect until the end of the day or during weekends. And then, when we finally do ponder what we've been through, we'll replay difficult conversations or problematic developments over and over.

Attention flows where energy goes, and by repeatedly replaying these scenarios, our primal brain and amygdala switch on, causing confusion and making us overthink things and create negative 'what ifs.'

2. We don't want to forget important tasks

Even though you've got something in your calendar, logged in a CRM or productivity app, our brain can still subconsciously think, 'I don't want you to forget these, so I'll keep them top of mind.'

However, this can once again activate our primal brain – which can only think in the present tense – leading us to feel like an issue needs to be resolved right now, even if it's 10:30 pm and you've already gone to bed.

This can trigger waves of stress and anxiety that can be difficult to shake off.

3. Looking for the elusive 'perfect' time for a break

The struggle with taking time off can be one of the hardest things about being in sales, but it isn't talked about enough. We all know the benefit of taking a break, but finding the right time to get away can be so difficult. There's the ever-present fear of either falling behind or losing momentum when you're on top of things.

We may find ourselves thinking and saying things like:

> 'I can't take time off. What will other people think?'
> 'If I take some days off, I'm going to miss out on leads.'
> 'I know it would only be one day away, but I'd have one less day to reach my quota.'

Along with the prospect of increased stress and burning out, not taking time off can lead to limiting beliefs. It's not uncommon for people in high-pressure jobs to convince themselves that the only way to be successful – or survive, for that matter – is by not taking regular leave.

4. Feeling part of the tribe

It's great when you've found a role and company that makes you feel valued and excited about their vision and where it's going. You can feel surprisingly connected, and see yourself as a key part in helping the business achieve its goals.

The challenge can be that you're so pumped about the possibilities, you develop a FOMO (fear of missing out) phobia, or concern over not wanting to let anybody down by being away from the office.

As a result, you may rarely take a day or two off, and struggle mightily with the idea of going on a two-week holiday. If you do manage to get up and go, you can feel the need to be constantly on email and messaging, when instead you should be stretched out poolside with a good book and a frosty drink.

5. You've got your self-worth too wrapped up in your job

As we've discussed previously, another reason we find it hard to switch off relates to our non-work identities.

If we come to associate too much of our self-worth and identity with our work, it becomes challenging to disconnect because we feel that's the only thing that defines us or gives us purpose.

As such, when we're not working we might feel a bit lost and struggle to find value or reward in non-work-related activity, such as simple rest and relaxation. If this resonates with you, I recommend focusing on the non-work identities exercise we detailed earlier, and finding non-work-related pursuits – hobbies, sports and other amusements – that bring you joy.

Inspirational Insights

Jacqueline de Gernier, SVP & Global Head of Business at consumer insights platform GWI, has a fascinating story to share.

Like many people in this book, I first became aware of Jacqui on LinkedIn, and we met at a roundtable I organised around best practice in sales training and mental wellbeing support .

Jacqui is a real advocate in this area, and once you hear her story you'll understand why.

"My brother and I were raised by our mum after my biological dad left us literally homeless and penniless," she told me. "My mum often went hungry to put food on the table for my brother and me, and free school dinners often provided us with our one hot meal per day. I was bullied at school for my clothes/glasses/shoes. Thankfully, most children today will not have to endure the humiliation of wearing National Health glasses, but it was a thing in the 1980s.

"My life took a more positive turn when my mum remarried when I was 11 years old. My wonderful step-dad became my one and only dad, and enabled me to thrive, go to university and believe that I could follow any path I wished to. While I would never wish my early experiences on anyone, I know that they shaped me and are a huge driver for me.

"As a female sales leader I have often worked in leadership teams where I am in the minority. Being a working mum often puts me in an even smaller group. My husband and I both work full time in fast-paced, demanding roles, and have both worked really hard over the years to ensure that we gave 100% at work while providing for our children too.

"In recent years, I've been happy to see working parents being more open about the challenges of juggling work and family, and organisations providing more flexible working policies.

"Unfortunately, my reality for the first 14 years of being a working parent was having to have childcare to ensure I could be in the office and available for meetings that might start at 8 or 8:30 am, or run over, to past 6 pm.

"It seems ridiculous now that I felt unable to put clear boundaries in place for when I could join meetings or calls, to allow me to have my children attend a nursery instead, or as they got older to do the school run myself rather than relying on childcare.

"At that time, I didn't see anyone else juggling the same commitments or having to create these boundaries. I therefore spent many years running fast, never saying no, giving everything I had left to my children in the evenings and weekends, and ultimately running on empty!

"I saw my physical and mental wellbeing suffer as a result, and have, on occasion, suffered from alopecia (a hair-loss condition), which is triggered by stress. COVID-19 and remote work changed all this for me, and has allowed me to re-define how and when I work and to be much more empowered.

"At my old company, Twilio, I also worked for a leadership team that prioritised the mental wellbeing of their teams and put their trust in you to organise your day and week in a way that set you up for success. It's really frustrating to reflect on how tough my experience of being a working parent was and how utterly avoidable this was.

"I hope by speaking about these issues, and shaping my teams and working cultures in a more inclusive way, I can ensure no other working parent has to have a similar experience. I've seen so many talented working mums opt out of their careers when some simple tweaks to their working hours and support for remote work would have allowed them to continue in their careers and been more supported.

"My advice? Speak up and be honest about how things at work may be impacting you and your family. Not being available 24/7 is not a sign of weakness or lack of commitment. Create time blocks in your calendar so you reinforce any boundaries you have during your day or week.

"Make sure you are taking time out during evenings and weekends — burning out is no use to anyone, and if you don't set boundaries for your time, you are almost certainly having issues working efficiently and prioritising.

"By applying this for myself I've developed better relationships with my family and have been there for all important events, provide them with emotional support and just generally be present a lot more.

"I've also felt more empowered at work to set guardrails and say no when needed, realising this did not impact my ability to drive results and to progress or get promoted. I generally feel like I 100% own my career and how I go about my work.

"My children are now 14 and 17 and I am proud of the stable, happy, prosperous life I have helped to provide them with, and the role model I can be to them both. But it has taken a huge amount of effort and at times has taken a big toll on my health."

Activity G1 —
Why do you find it difficult
to switch off?

The common theme in this book is awareness, and that applies here as well. If you find it difficult to switch off or take time away from work, take a moment to reflect on the above and note in the box below which of the five points most resonate with you.

This will serve you well, when done along with the other ways of challenging your thoughts and actions that we've discussed throughout the book.

What makes it difficult for you to switch off?

Your Three Key Takeaways:

1) You can struggle to switch off due to a lack of time for reflection, preventing you from processing daily experiences and emotions effectively.

2) The subconscious fear of forgetting important tasks can keep people mentally engaged even during leisure time, contributing to stress and difficulty relaxing.

3) The quest for the 'perfect' time to take breaks can create stress, as people worry about falling behind targets or missing out on opportunities, leading to reluctance to switch off.

CHAPTER 32

Recharging and Relieving the Pressure of Sales

Now that we've explored ways to become more mindful of how to manage, protect and preserve your energy, it's time to focus on something equally important: how you recharge your energy.

Let's revisit the phone battery analogy. No matter how well you do at watching how long you use your phone, or what you use it for, if you don't charge it, it'll run out of juice. It's important to find ways to regularly recharging your 'human' battery, including creating your own recharge stations.

Imagine these as actions that proactively and reactively help you avoid reaching unhealthy levels of stress that can lead to burnout, or reacting in ways you look back on and regret. Here's a bit more about these and when you might use them.

Proactive Recharge Stations

Imagine it's a Saturday afternoon, and you're going out with friends in the evening. You see that your phone battery is at around 20% capacity. With the big night ahead, you'd definitely be charging it, right? Even though it has some battery time left, you know that by 10:00 tonight it'll be dead.

We see this as a no-brainer, but we often don't apply the same logic to our own personal energy stores. We often wait until we 'need' a break or a holiday before we take one, or until the end of a grueling day before we recharge.

Often, when we get to this point, we've been operating in battery-saving mode, perhaps procrastinating on tasks and not fully focused or performing anywhere near our best.

These proactive recharge stations are there to use before we feel like we need them, because the more we tap into them, the less likely we'll reach that point of real need.

You can factor recharging into your daily routine, just as you'd plan on time for prospecting or industry research. They only have to take 5-10 minutes each, and can be part of your non-negotiables.

Your Reactive Recharge Stations

Your reactive recharge stations are there as a sort of emergency 'break glass' solution. They're the ones you use when you've had a moment in the day that caused distress, frustration or any kind of emotion.

It could be an unexpected, troublesome email, a deal that gets pushed back, or something difficult happening in your personal life. These recharge opportunities are there as a quick resource, to help get you get back into a healthy headspace, reset and recover.

Without that, it's easy to react irrationally or engage in negative self-talk when the unexpected happens, as we discussed in relation to harnessing your emotional rollercoaster.

For example:
- After reading that unexpected email, thinking, 'My day is ruined now'
- Snapping at a colleague who keeps coming back to ask you questions
- Telling colleagues, 'We're never going to hit the target now' after a deal of yours is postponed, and then sulking around the office all day

Your reactive stations are your go-to tools in these moments, to help reset yourself before any judgements or reactions.

Let's say you've just had a one-on-one with your manager where you received some blunt feedback you weren't expecting. Make an agreement with yourself: 'I'm not going to snap-judge this. I'm not going to create irrational stories in my head. I'm going to use one of my reactive recharges, and then come back and reflect on this, focus on what I can control, let the feedback digest and carry on with my day.'

By utilising your reactive recharge stations, you're training your mind and giving it the space to respond logically, rather than react irrationally, which will further improve your self-regulation and avoid creating limiting beliefs.

So, the next time you find yourself in one of those moments, give yourself time to use a reactive tap.

Proactive recharge stations	Reactive recharge stations
Going for a daily walk before or after work, or at lunch time.	Taking five minutes outside, away from technology and people, to get some fresh air.
Listening to a music playlist you've created every morning, before cold-calling.	Activating the 90-Second Window.
Leaving your phone somewhere outside your bedroom at night, when you're asleep.	Speaking to someone who will give you space to talk, but not exacerbate how you're feeling.
Reviewing weekly wins every Friday afternoon.	The Five Senses Exercise.
Planning a weekend day once a month for a self-care solo date.	Listening to a playlist you've created specifically for work, to recharge and reinvigorate yourself.

Your proactive and reactive recharges can be the same activity, but just used in a different context. For example, you may use The Five Senses Exercise every morning when you wake up proactively, but also reactively after a tough call.

Activity G2 —
Identifying Your Proactive
& Reactive Recharges

Now, run through some of the proactive and reactive refresh steps you can start implementing (or continue using) in your day and week, to ensure that you're sufficiently recharging your energy.

Proactive recharge stations	Reactive recharge stations

Your Three Key Takeaways:

1) Establish proactive recharge stations that you incorporate into your routine, regardless of stress levels and demands on your time, ensuring they don't build to unhealthy or unsustainable levels.

2) Create reactive recharge stations for emergency use when unexpected stressors arise, helping you reset, develop self-regulation and avoid negative reactions.

3) The more proactive recharges you use, the less reactive you'll need to be.

CHAPTER 33

How to Unplug and Boost Your Performance in the Present

Now that we've covered why it can be difficult to switch off and take time away from work, let's get into practical ways of addressing this. This part will cover tools you can use to support switching off in the present, and during evenings and weekends.

You may want to include these in your non-negotiables, or those proactive and reactive recharges each day or week.

Let's start by recalling two common reasons, covered earlier, why we find it hard to switch off:

- We're so busy in our day, we don't have time or space to reflect
- We don't want to forget important tasks and fall behind

Here's a handy tool you can adopt as a daily or weekly habit: The Brain Dump.

The Brain Dump

This is something you can do at the end of each working day, and it only takes 5-10 minutes. It's a tool that allows you to reflect on your day, acknowledge what still needs to be done, celebrate your wins, identify challenges, and plan how you'll overcome them tomorrow.

Knowing that you have a plan and feel prepared brings peace of mind, which makes it easier for your brain to switch off.

We'll use a grid to plot this out below, but I also recommend taking a pen and paper to write it down instead of typing, so it's more visceral and visual.

Divide your page into four quadrants:

#1 Pending:

This is where you jot down everything on your mind for tomorrow (or next week) – outstanding tasks, to-do lists, worries, essentially anything and everything.

You can even include non-work items because the more you unload now, the better you'll feel. The more you write down here, the less your brain will feel the need to store and remember.

#2 Wins:

Think about what you achieved today that you're proud of. Focus on your actions rather than just the outcomes.

This is a chance to acknowledge your accomplishments and give yourself a pat on the back. It's all about self-reflection, as we discussed earlier.

#3 Challenges:

We all have those days where we don't feel entirely ourselves, or stress gets the best of us. We rarely take the time to dig deeper and understand why this happens, which means it's likely to keep on happening.

What hindered your productivity today? Did you struggle with anything that needs closure before the evening? Writing down these challenges allows us to focus on the next section (solutions), and avoid dwelling on them or keeping the feeling as a static emotion.

#4 Solutions:

Now that you've identified the bumps in the road during your day, it's time to brainstorm solutions, to help preempt or overcome them tomorrow.

By doing this, you instantly feel reassured that you have a plan to move forward with, rather than dwelling on what hindered your productivity today.

It's about finding proactive ways to make those small improvements each day, and prevent a one-off challenge from becoming a common occurrence over time if left unaddressed.

Here's an example of what this could look like:

#1 Pending	#2 Wins
• Schedule meeting with Tim • Book a networking session with Ori • Call dentist for check-up • Arrange weekend plans with friends • Review call before meeting tomorrow afternoon • Plan my focus time for next week • Ask for feedback from my manager about a specific call	• Got out for a walk before work • Identified 15 new potential prospects • Delivered an effective demo • Learnt about the Pomodoro Technique to help me with time management • Booked a holiday • Avoided my phone during focus time
#3 Challenges	**#4 Solutions**
• Got caught up in Slack messages that didn't involve me • Realised that I dwelt on a cold call for longer than I wanted to • Found myself getting asked questions throughout my time for LinkedIn research	• Close down Slack tomorrow during focus times • Try one of my reactive recharges tomorrow if that happens again • Pre-empt my colleagues by advising when I'll be free for questions, and establish urgency of queries before answering

Activity G3 —
The Brain Dump Exercise

Now it's your turn to give it a go. This typically works best just before the end of your working day, so perhaps schedule some time in your calendar now for that.

#1 Pending	#2 Wins
#3 Challenges	**#4 Solutions**

Action to implement the habit: See what you notice in the evening, and the next day, as a result of doing this. If it proves useful, set a daily reminder – or weekly, if you prefer doing it on that basis – to build the habit and support you in switching off.

Along with the Brain Dump exercise, here are three other things that help you switch off more effectively in the evenings and over weekends.

1. Get outside

This one works particularly well when you've been working from home. Getting outside at the beginning or end of your day is a great way to break it up and give yourself space to prepare or reflect.

An added bonus is that by mixing up your environment you may find that your headspace becomes clearer. Some of my best ideas have come to me when I'm away from my desk, liberated from calls, notification pings and computer tabs.

Being outdoors helps me process those tough moments in the day. Moving my body prevents me from getting stuck in my chair, overthinking situations and replaying them in my head.

Getting out, and getting in motion, disrupts the repeating thought patterns of the primal brain. Varying your route will keep your rational brain engaged, preventing you from going into autopilot mode, which can defeat the purpose of venturing into the great outdoors.

Along the way, the fresh air, natural light, sounds, smells and unstructured, free-flowing mobility can all be remarkably restorative.

2. Schedule your own deadlines

We all know that our most productive working day ever is the day before we go on holiday. You're absolutely in the zone, getting everything done because you know it's your last chance before going away.

Creating a similar approach to your work-a-day week can be just as effective. Scheduling things for immediately after work – a workout class, a dinner reservation or walking your neighbour's dog – drives you to address matters at work more efficiently and get them done on time.

By doing this, you give yourself a deadline to work towards and avoid Parkinson's Law, which says that the more time you have to do something, the longer you'll take to do it.

This doesn't mean you should try this every day of the week, but it helps avoid consistently working late, switches off your mind, helps nurture those non-work identities and transitions you into something else.

Even when you work late or on weekends, give yourself a deadline. Instead of simply being resigned to 'working late tonight,' set a specific time to finish, like 7 pm. That will ensure that you're far more efficient with the additional hours you do spend at the grindstone.

3. Removing work apps on the weekend

I used to find myself on a Sunday, sitting on the sofa, watching TV, and after a while I'd realise I was mindlessly scrolling through my work emails, Slack or LinkedIn.

It had become a habit, and at times I didn't even notice that I was doing it. This effectively kept my brain in work mode through evenings and weekends, making me feel like I hadn't really had a break.

One simple way to break this habit is to make it harder to access work apps. Literally deleting them from your phone at end-of-day Friday is a great way to do this. It prevents you from being just a click away from unnecessarily checking emails or Slack, or being interrupted by work-related notifications – that incessant pinging that demands an immediate look – when you're trying to enjoy time with friends or your partner.

You might worry that *not* checking emails gives you more anxiety, even on holiday. I can understand that. For those who feel this way, give yourself a designated window to check them instead of having unrestricted access.

It could be a 15-minute slot on Saturday morning, and then 30 minutes on Sunday evening, or a brief daily check-in while on vacation. Find a schedule that works for you, but make it intentional and avoid being at your phone's beck and call.

If you're convinced that your best work involves sending emails or messages in the evening and on weekends, I'm not here to stop you. But I'd strongly urge you to use the 'schedule send' feature.

I know you and others out there may work at different times and don't expect an immediate response. However, helpful disclaimers, like 'One for Monday' or 'When you get back' are often buried in the email itself.

This of course means the recipient will have already seen the email, opened it, read through it, started thinking about it and switched on to that topic. By scheduling the send time, you can eliminate all of that, so make use of this feature and avoid unnecessary interruptions.

Inspirational Insights

Charlotte Johnson, an Account Executive at Salesloft, has firsthand experience handling this. I first became aware of Charly through seeing her practical and insightful tips on LinkedIn. She's always very open and honest with her posts, so I knew she'd have a relatable story and good advice to share in this guide.

"I've suffered from anxiety for a long time," she told me. "Everything from panic attacks and insomnia, to not being able to leave the house. Combining this with a sales role has not been easy, but over the years I've gone to therapy, tried meditation techniques and implemented some of the tools mentioned below, which have helped me better understand how to manage my anxiety monster.

"In the past, overworking is something I would be really guilty of doing. I would put all my energy and attention into work, starting early and logging off late, while constantly checking emails, Slack, LinkedIn, etc.

"Work literally became my life, which would lead to burnout. From overworking, I sometimes wouldn't leave the house for days, which also spiked my anxiety. I'd have an odd anxiety outbreak when doing certain tasks alone, such as going to the shops, which sounds insane, but it would be heightened when I would have days of not leaving the house.

"On top of this, with all my energy being work-related, it led to me also massively attached to the outcome of every single call and interaction I had. I would even dream about work constantly, which led to insomnia.

"I wanted to change this, so I started thinking how I could better separate work from my personal life. It's funny how, since setting clear boundaries for myself, my confidence and success have increased while massively decreasing my anxiety.

"I work normal hours and am strict with these times. Previously, I'd do a discovery call at 9 pm if it meant getting closer to target. But now, unless urgent, I stick to my 9-5 hours. And limiting my hours has also made me more organized, as I need to get my work completed in this time. When I'm in my personal hours I cannot check work apps, as I've actually now deleted them from my phone.

"Here are two things that help me remove work thoughts from my brain:

1) Daily to-do lists, jotting down EVERYTHING I need to be doing that's work related. Previously these work tasks would just be floating around in my head, so without realising it I was always thinking about work.

2) Mind techniques - This has helped, especially with my insomnia. I have a technique for removing topics from my brain. I simply close my eyes and I see my brain as a room. All the thoughts are objects — the bigger the thought, the bigger the object. And in my brain room with the objects, there is also a small 'me' who can push these objects out of the room.

"So in my head I physically push objects I don't want to think about out, and this helps when I can't switch off from work. I've not heard of many who do this, but it's something I do daily.

"Setting these boundaries has made me a better worker and happier person. It's reduced my anxiety and stress, and I'm sleeping again. This was a big plus, as my insomnia was really bad. I'm now seeing friends and family more, too.

"Overall, I'm a much happier and more relaxed human, which makes me better at work and a more fun person to be around. My advice would be that if you're feeling like I was before, share how you're feeling.

"You're not the only person going through this, and talking about how you're feeling can help lift this heavy weight. Don't be afraid to seek help. Therapy changed my life, but it is almost a topic people try to keep hidden."

Your Three Key Takeaways:

1) Think about detaching from technology when looking to switch off, and instead toggle onto things that recharge you.

2) Use the Brain Dump exercise regularly to reflect on your day, create a plan for the next one and reduce the chances of it consuming your mind when you're away from work.

3) Switching off can help you become more effective when you switch back on.

CHAPTER 34

Pit Stops and Resting Hard

It's great to have the tools and understanding of how to switch off during after-hours and on weekends, but what about when you need to hit that off switch for a longer period? This might be for going away on holiday, doing a staycation, or simply enjoying being home one afternoon without a schedule to stick to.

As we covered earlier, one of the biggest reasons you might find it difficult to take time off is that it never feels like the 'perfect time.' But remember, there's no such thing as the perfect time.

I want you to imagine that sales is like being in a Formula 1 automobile race. You're in a constant fight for position, and throughout the race you know you need to take 2-3 pit stops. For our purposes, those could be a weekend away, a long holiday abroad, etc.

Taking these stops will mean drivers temporarily drop back a few places in the race, but they can be the game-changer. It's a moment to give things a quick once-over, make needed adjustments, and avoid having their tyres burn out and running out of fuel.

Look at your time off like pit stops; something essential to your long-term strategy and sustainable success.

When you're thinking of taking leave, you may often focus on what you could lose out on as a result. Instead, here are three things to consider:

1. What's the impact of not taking that break?
We can be so busy thinking about all the things that could happen from being away (losing out on leads, endless emails when we get back, less time to make quota) that we lose sight of the impact of not doing so.

The repercussions of not taking that holiday could be:

> Greater risk of burnout
> Increase in stress and feeling more frustrated
> Neglecting a non-work identity (travelling, skiing, learning new guitar tunes, spending time with family/partner/friends)
> Developing the limiting belief that you can never take time off

Investing more of your time pondering this question – what happens if you don't break away now and then – creates a more balanced view, rather than just focusing on what you may lose out on when you're away.

2. What will you be gaining as a result of taking time off?
If we just focus on what we're losing out on, our primal brain will of course amplify that. What can really help build a healthier mindset towards these pit stops is focusing on what you'll be gaining on your time off.

It could be:

> Coming back feeling recharged and with fresh ideas
> Spending time exploring the world and learning more about yourself
> Quality time with your partner, kids or other family members
> Giving your body and mind a break from the daily stress

This is also a good question to think through when you come back from holiday or a long weekend, to reinforce why you did it in the first place.

3. How can I become more comfortable with taking time off?

Echoing Chapter 1, where we looked at confirmation bias and limiting beliefs, asking this type of question gets us thinking about how to solve a challenge, rather than defaulting to, 'I can't afford to take time off.'

For example, asking this question could mean that you:

> Find a trusted colleague or two to direct emails to when off
> Focus on the first two questions above – the impact of taking, or not taking a break – to reinforce the benefit
> Plan for down time in advance, so you build a healthy pipeline to carry you through your break
> Aim for target months or weeks where you feel it will be quieter than usual, making a getaway more manageable

Getting more comfortable with figuring out solutions to your time-away concerns, rather than fostering a limiting belief that stays with you, can make a real difference.

You don't necessarily have to answer these questions in order every time you think about a getaway, but each holds value.

Another tip that can help you decide to take those pit stops, and avoiding constantly thinking about work when you're off, is making a 'comeback plan' for when you return to the office. Whether it's a long weekend, a week or a few, this will help you feel more prepared for re-entry.

It also helps avoid those anxious thoughts of uncertainty that can bubble up near the end of your holiday, as you begin to worry about what you'll do when you first get back.

This plan can simply involve time-blocking your diary for the first couple of days, with key catch-up and housekeeping tasks, giving yourself some small goals for that week, and revisiting/revising your plan for reaching your target for the month or quarter.

All of this will soothe your primal brain, so if you do start worrying when you're away, you can quickly look at your calendar and say, 'We've got this planned already.'

Psyche Success Stories — Sham & Reducing Burnout

Let's take a look at Sham, who had a great internal brand as an Account Manager with a scale-up CRM software business. Sham was always consistent, and by his own admission never a top performer, but he always met expectations. He was the person others spoke about as a good example, but Sham had a problem.

He'd rarely touch his annual leave, and under the surface it was impacting him. What others didn't know was that Sham was always on the cusp of burnout, spending most weekends at home, sleeping. It wasn't that he didn't want to take time off, but rather his perception that if he did, he wouldn't hit target. This was a classic case of a limiting belief.

After we had some one-on-one sessions together, Sham started to challenge this limiting belief, acknowledging the risks of stress and burnout. We worked through the 'Notice it. Name it. Neutralise it' tool covered here earlier, along with the vacation/no vacation rationale questions detailed in this part of the book. Sham also spent some time reflecting on his non-work identities and non-negotiables.

This helped him shift the focus from potential losses to gains, realising the benefits of down time for personal and professional wellbeing. Sham began to take more blocks of time off, starting small. Sure enough, he noticed that he felt more refreshed and present when outside of work, and his job performance ramped up. In fact, he finished in President's Club that year.

By taking time out to switch off, he was more present and efficient when he switched back on.

Activity G4 —
The Impact of Not Taking A Break

Think about how the questions apply to you. Whether you have some time off booked already, or are thinking of doing so but are hesitant, this line of self-inquiry should prove helpful.

1. What's the impact of not taking that break?

2. What will you be gaining as a result of taking time off?

3. How can you become more comfortable with taking time off?

Rest as Hard as You Work

I attended a New Year's Eve gathering hosted by the artist Notes to Strangers (aka Andy Leek) at the end of 2022. Andy creates short, meaningful messages that he places around cities for people to randomly come across, all with the purpose of bringing a moment of joy and a smile to their face.

When I arrived, we were invited to pick out a few of these messages to share, and one instantly caught my eye: 'Rest as Hard as You Work.' So, I grabbed it. If you've seen me virtually since then, you might have noticed it in the background, and I often get asked about it. Sometimes it's these kinds of sceptical questions:

- 'Does that mean you shouldn't work as much?'
- 'Isn't that the problem these days – the work ethic has been lost?'
- 'I don't enjoy doing nothing; it doesn't make me feel productive.'

One of the reasons this message resonates with me is that it sparks an interesting debate about what we mean by 'hard work.'

Working hard is often associated with the amount of time we put in, but someone can work harder than others without spending 12 hours a day at it. It doesn't say 'Rest as *much* as you work.'

What the message is really about is ensuring that you're thinking about how you're resting. It's not just something that happens by accident, but is instead something you're conscious of what type is best for you. It's all very well working as hard as you can, but without a plan on how you recharge and reset, it's not sustainable.

This message also brings up the way we perceive the notion of rest. I've spoken to many people who find kicking back difficult because they see it as unproductive or feel guilty about not working more. This can especially be the case when they compare themselves to others they see online.

But rest doesn't have to mean doing nothing. That can be part of it, and there are times when that can be the perfect remedy, but it's not the whole picture. Rest can be just as proactive as working.

Going for a hike, exercising, having lunch with a friend or playing a musical instrument can all be forms of rest. Often, we sacrifice rest because we think it means doing nothing and being still. By reframing rest as something that can also be an activity, we can give it more importance and avoid sacrificing it for work-related activities.

Inspirational Insights

Let's hear from Cinzia Soro, who works in the customer success space. I first met Cinzia when she was at Meta, where I led a number of workshops and did one-on-one coaching.

Cinzia's story centres around a newfound mantra of hers: 'It's not happening TO you, it's happening FOR you.'

"After some recent changes in life, I focused on landing the type of job I truly desired," she told me. "Not just in terms of a role and company fit, but on a personal level, that would allow me to live the life I want now.

"I was determined to find a position that would allow me to truly enjoy and effectively disconnect from work in the way that my experience taught me is best for me: traveling, exploring new cultures, and being able to move between my two homes — one where I grew up with my family, and the other in London, where I've created my new home over the last decade.

"Now, I'm grateful to have secured a new position that enables me to do that, as I can work remotely from abroad whenever I choose.

"While the position is temporary, its impact on my wellbeing and work performance has been incredible so far, and for me much more important than stability.

"I think this opportunity highlights the importance of a job that allows individuals to disconnect in ways that suit them best — where my preference for working from different places is just an example — and how this is essential for staying productive, succeeding in a role and leading a ful-filling, balanced life."

Your Three Key Takeaways:

1) Strategic Breaks: Don't wait for the perfect time; there isn't one. Breaks are like pit stops — crucial for long-term success and avoiding burnout.

2) Impact and Gains: Assess the impact of not taking a break and focus on gains from taking them.

3) Proactive Rest: 'Rest as Hard as You Work.' Reframe rest as engaging in activities that rejuvenate your mind and body for sustainable success.

Conclusion

To wrap things up, I have one last story to share with you, and I'll start with the conclusion:

No matter how hard you train, you're still going to get punched in the head.

A few years ago, I started boxing and dedicated myself to training several times a week. I noticed improvements in my fitness and technique, but one aspect continued to bother me: getting punched. In my mind, I believed that the more skilled I became, I should get to a point where I don't get punched in the head.

However, one day my coach said to me, "No matter how hard you train, you're still going to get punched in the head. The better you become, the fewer hits you'll take, but don't expect to reach a point where you never get hit. This training is not only about reducing the chances of being hit, it's also about teaching you how to handle it when it does happen."

This is the message I want to emphasize at the end of this guide, as it's so applicable to how you look at your wellbeing and sales performance. No matter how much you work on your mindset and salescraft, you're still going to have times where things don't go to plan, you start over-thinking things or you feel stressed and anxious.

But by working on your mindset and utilizing the tools and techniques covered in this book, you can decrease the frequency of these moments popping up in your day. And, most importantly, you can change the way you respond. You can't always control what happens to you, but you can control how you respond to it, in ways that are far more rational and effective than a rash, knee-jerk reaction.

In doing so, you prevent those moments from sabotaging your week, weekend, month or quarterly performance.

So, let's briefly recap what we've covered in this guide.

In Part A, we focused on mastering your mind through better understanding your self-talk, the limiting beliefs we can create, and how to notice, name and neutralise them. Along with that, there's the importance of identifying your controllables and the value of relabelling your familiar zone.

In Part B, we delved into the emotional rollercoaster of sales and how to better understand your emotions, the signals they can produce to support you, and tools to help you have a measured response, rather than impulsive reaction, to them.

Part C was dedicated to a commonly used, but misunderstood, word: motivation. We looked at how to better recognise the origins and direction of yours. This involved identifying your hospital, bricks and walls, along with how having a surfer mentality and focusing on kickstarting motivation, rather than waiting for it, can put you more in control of yours.

Part D looked at redefining failure in sales, the importance that resilience plays and addressing four of the common myths associated with it. And, we discussed the three different types of knockbacks you can face, and how to better embrace them and seek feedback to support you in your continual growth and development.

Part E centred on unleashing your inner sales champion, how to focus on healthy comparisons and the immense value of building the habit of self-reflection. Along with this, we talked about how to focus on courage instead of confidence, and better understand imposter syndrome and the tools to leverage it.

Part F was all about managing and protecting your energy, to ensure a more consistent approach, by becoming more conscious of the stages and hidden causes of burnout. To help with this, we examined how to set healthy boundaries, the importance of your non-negotiables and how to become more comfortable with saying no.

Finally, Part G was dedicated to ways of switching off and recharging effectively. We spoke of the reasons why it can feel difficult to do this, introduced proactive and reactive recharges, and touched on ways to switch off in the short term and long run. That's all critical to maintaining a healthy mind and body while building a sustainable approach to your sales career.

How to Cement Your Learning

So, how do you make this stick? How do you avoid this guide becoming just another thing you've read, found useful, but never picked up or utilised again?

In the opening pages, I started out with some thoughts on how to make best use of this material. That bears repeating. So here, in the closing pages, let's recap some of the ways you can continue to work on this.

1. **Be proactive with the tools before you 'need' them.**

   The more proactive you are, the less reactive you'll need to be. Embedding these tools in your habits and routines means they'll be there, at your fingertips, when necessary. As with presenting your product or handling objections, practice them ahead of time to bake them into your thought process and approach.

2. **Be patient with yourself when working on these areas.**

   Some will come easier than others, but recognise the value of the ones that don't. Just like when you started cold calling or trying to close deals, the more you did it, the more familiar it became. And like those achy muscles after a good run or workout, the mechanics of working through them represent progress. Stay consistent with them.

3. Use this guide like a playlist.

Think of this guide like your go-to playlist. Just as you return to your favorite tracks to shift your mood or find inspiration, you can revisit this guide whenever you need a quick refresher on how to handle situations as they unfold.

4. Create anchor reminders.

Creating visual reminders (anchors) of specific tools and tips can further support you in developing your craft. Here are some suggestions for this:

> Use post-it notes and stick them on your laptop, with a visual icon to remind you to check in on them.

> Put reminders in your calendar to prompt you at certain times.

> Tell a colleague, close friend, partner or manager of something you're working on, and ask them to regularly check-in with you on it.

Thank You

So, that's a wrap.

First, I want to thank you for picking up this guide and working through it. I hope it serves you well in and outside of your sales career, as I'm sure you can see how many of these tools transcend your work life.

And, I want you to thank yourself. It's admirable that you're investing in yourself, focusing on you, and taking care of 'number one.' As you've read here, we don't give ourselves enough credit for the things we do. You reading this book has been an exercise in self-gratitude, so I want you to take a moment to thank yourself for going through and utilising this guide.

The world of sales has evolved, and will continue to do so, which makes it all the more important to be conscious of taking care of your mindset and wellbeing. We as a community are getting better at shining a light on this, and by using the tools in this guide, makes you part of that movement.

Whether it's with your colleagues, prospects, customers, family or friends, share these insights and activities, and talk about them. The more we do this, the more we normalise this self-help as part and parcel of sales and the better we'll become, not just in performance, but also in our headspace.

It's been an absolute pleasure writing this guide, and I hope you've enjoyed reading it.

Stay mindful,
Chris

It would be great to hear your thoughts,
reflections and takeaways from reading this guide.

Feel free to get in touch with me at
chris.hatfield@salespsyche.co.uk
or connect with me on LinkedIn.

You'll find me sharing regular tips on those platforms,
and you can take advantage of my self-paced online
courses on topics I've covered in this guide.

If you want to get in touch to discuss
working together, reach out via email, LinkedIn
or at **www.salespsyche.co.uk**

I work with individuals in one-on-one coaching,
provide workshop programmes, teach online courses
and present keynote talks.

I also run a weekly London based run club,
Run Your Mind, that is focused on taking care of your
mental wellbeing. If you want to get into running or are
a runner, come join us. You can find us on Instagram
(**@runyourmindclub**).

The Playbook

Have you ever finished reading a book and thought, 'Great, I've learnt so much,' but been confused about how to mix, match and leverage the various insights, tips and tools in specific situations?

Perhaps you want a go-to resource when faced with a new or uncertain situation, for guidance on some practical tools to support you.

Fear not. Along with the scenarios mentioned throughout this guide, here is a playbook of situations you may face in your sales role. For each, you'll find 2-3 helpful activities we discussed.

This can come in handy in your role as a salesperson, or for a manager to use in coaching sessions or team workshops.

Here are various scenarios and the associated tools (with page numbers).

 A reminder that you can find all the exercise worksheets from The Playbook online, using the QR code here.

Theme	Scenario
Thoughts and beliefs	Thinking a call or demo won't go well
	Wondering if you did or said something wrong
	Comparison with others leading you to feel negatively about yourself
	Feeling you don't deserve to be in your role or successful
	Tracking behind target
Emotions	Feeling like you're not doing 'enough' or are 'behind'
	Starting to feel burnt out
	Feeling stressed at end of month or quarter
	Having a short fuse and often reacting negatively
Motivation	Struggling with motivation after a long period in role
	Hesitating starting something new
Knockbacks/ change	Finding it difficult to deal with change
	Missing target or losing a big deal

Tool 1	Page	Tool 2	Page	Tool 3	Page
A4	47	B1	55	B1	88
A3	40	A5	55	E8	268
E1	221	E2	226	E3	232
E6	255	E8	268	E3	232
A6	65	A1	21	B1	88
F5	312	E2	226	A6	65
F3	295	G2	338	G4	357
B2	97	A4	47	A6	65
B2	97	A5	55	A1	21
C1	115	C2	123	C5	148
A7	72	B1	88	C1	115
A4	47	A7	72	B1	88
D3	186	A6	65	C5	148

Theme	Scenario
Personal development & growth	Unaware of what makes you good at what you do
	Get defensive when receiving feedback
	Want to build a growth mindset
	Lacking confidence in new sales role
Time/energy management	Want to work on time management and planning
	Want to be able to more effectively switch off from work
Career development	Career planning
	Wanting to improve in a specific aspect of your role
	Starting a new role or being promoted
	After a successful deal, month or quarter
Public speaking	Apprehensive about posting content online
	Anxious about presenting

Tool 1	Page	Tool 2	Page	Tool 3	Page
D4	202	E3	232	E4	236
D4	196	D4	202	B1	88
A1	21	D4	196	D4	202
A1	21	D4	202	E5	245
F5	312	F6	320	G3	344
G2	338	G1	332	G3	344
C1	115	C3	132		
C3	132	E3	232	C1	115
C1	115	B1	88	F4	305
C4	140	E4	236	F3	295
A2		C2	123	E5	245
E5	245	A4	47	B2	97

Theme	Scenario
Resilience	Overall Resilience
	Challenge
	Commitment
	Personalisation
	Permanence
	Pervasiveness
Imposter Syndrome	Overall Imposter Syndrome
	The Expert
	The Perfectionist
	The Natural Genius
	The Workaholic

Tool 1	Page	Tool 2	Page	Tool 3	Page
D1	176	E3	232		
D2	186	A6	65	A4	47
C1	115	C2	123	F2	292
A3	40	A6	65	D4	196
A1	21	C5	148	E4	236
B3	97	G3	344	A5	55
E6	255	E7	258	E8	268
A3	40	A5	55	D2	186
F6	320	F5	312	C4	140
A7	72	E5	245	A5	55
F2	292	G4	357	G2	338

References

1. Gartner. "Gartner Sales Survey Finds Nearly 90 Percent of Sellers Feel Burned Out from Work." August 30, 2022. https://www.gartner.com/en/newsroom/press-releases/2022-08-30-gartner-sales-survey-finds-nearly-90-percent-of-selle

2. Shawn Achor, The Happiness Advantage: How a Positive Brain Fuels Success in Work and Life (New York: Crown Business, 2010), 41.

3. Colloca, Luana, and Damien Finniss. 2012. "Nocebo Effects, Patient-Clinician Communication, and Therapeutic Outcomes." JAMA 307 (6): 567-568.

4. Kabat-Zinn, Jon. *Full Catastrophe Living: Using the Wisdom of Your Body and Mind to Face Stress, Pain, and Illness*. New York: Delta, 1990. Beck, Judith S. *Cognitive Therapy: Basics and Beyond*. New York: Guilford Press, 1995.

5. Piaget, Jean. *The Construction of Reality in the Child*. New York: Basic Books, 1954.

6. TalentSmartEQ. "Increasing Your Salary with Emotional Intelligence." Accessed November 4, 2023. https://www.talentsmarteq.com/articles/increasing-your-salary-with-emotional-intelligence/.

7. TalentSmartEQ. "Increasing Your Salary with Emotional Intelligence." Accessed November 4, 2023. https://www.talentsmarteq.com/emotional-intelligence-can-boost-your-career-and-save-your-life/#:~:text=TalentSmartEQ%20tested%20emotional%20intelligence%20alongside,in%20all%20types%20of%20jobs.

8. Daniel Goleman, *Emotional Intelligence: Why It Can Matter More Than IQ* (New York: Bantam Books, 1995).

9. Peter Salovey and John D. Mayer, "Emotional Intelligence," Imagination, Cognition and Personality 9, no. 3 (1990): 185-211.

10. Deloitte. *Managing Emotions*. Series on Empowered Well Being. Deloitte, 2020. Accessed August 10, 2023. https://www2.deloitte.com/content/dam/Deloitte/us/Images/Misc/infographic/managing-emotions-infographic.pdf.

11. Jill Bolte Taylor, *My Stroke of Insight* (New York: Viking, 2008).

12. Kabat-Zinn, Jon. *Full Catastrophe Living: Using the Wisdom of Your Body and Mind to Face Stress, Pain, and Illness*. New York: Delta, 1990. Beck, Judith S. *Cognitive Therapy: Basics and Beyond*. New York: Guilford Press, 1995.

13. Deci, Edward L., and Richard M. Ryan. *Intrinsic Motivation and Self-Determination in Human Behavior.* New York: Plenum Press, 1985.

14. Deci, Edward L. "Effects of Externally Mediated Rewards on Intrinsic Motivation." Journal of Personality and Social Psychology 18, no. 1 (1971): 105-115.

15. Masten, Ann S. 2001. "Ordinary Magic: Resilience Processes in Development." American Psychologist 56 (3): 227-238.

16. Folkman, Susan, and Richard S. Lazarus. 1984. Stress, Appraisal, and Coping. New York: Springer Publishing Company.

17. Kahneman, Daniel, and Amos Tversky. 1979. "Prospect Theory: An Analysis of Decision under Risk." Econometrica 47 (2): 263-291.

18. Cohen, Sheldon, and Thomas A. Wills. 1985. "Stress, Social Support, and the Buffering Hypothesis." Psychological Bulletin 98 (2): 310-357.

19. Smith, Adam, and Brian Jones. *Resilience: Theory and Practice.* New York: Routledge, 2010. Brown, Celia. *The Gifts of Imperfection: Let Go of Who You Think You're Supposed to Be and Embrace Who You Are.* Center City, MN: Hazelden Publishing, 2015.

20. Carlsen, A. "The Three Types of Failure and How to Handle Them," *Forbes,* May 22, 2017, accessed June 10, 2024, https://www.forbes.com/sites/ashleystahl/2017/05/22/the-three-types-of-failure-and-how-to-handle-them/?sh=7de968742063.

21. Douglas Stone and Sheila Heen, *Thanks for the Feedback: The Science and Art of Receiving Feedback Well* (New York: Viking Penguin, 2014).

22. Festinger, Leon. "A Theory of Social Comparison Processes." *Human Relations* 7, no. 2 (1954): 117-140.

23. Valerie Young, *The Secret Thoughts of Successful Women: Why Capable People Suffer from the Impostor Syndrome and How to Thrive in Spite of It* (New York: Crown Business, 2011): 40-41.

24. Freudenberger, Herbert J. "Staff Burn-Out." *Journal of Social Issues* 30, no. 1 (1974): 159-165. Maslach, Christina, and Susan E. Jackson. "The Measurement of Experienced Burnout." *Journal of Occupational Behaviour* 2, no. 2 (1981): 99-113.

25. Vanessa K. Bohns. 2016. (Mis)understanding our influence over others: A review of the underestimation of compliance effect, Current Directions in Psychological Science. 25:119-123. (DOI:10.1177/0963721415628011)

Book blurb

The world of sales continues to evolve rapidly, with advances and investment into tools designed to make salespeople more efficient and effective. Yet, despite this, the biggest tool in a salesperson's locker is still being neglected. The elephant in the room: their mind. You can have all the tools and technology for your role, but if you don't understand how to develop and take care of your mind, you'll be in for a constant battle.

Sales Psyche is a transformative resource to address this. It's a guide that bridges the gap between becoming a more effective salesperson and developing your mindset and mental wellbeing.

The seven parts of this guide cover every aspect of doing this. We'll cover tackling limiting beliefs, reframing stress, addressing the myths of motivation, building resilience, becoming your own biggest champion and combating burnout, the silent sales killer.

This guide aims to address unspoken challenges in sales, offering essential insights, stories and tools to unlock your full potential. It goes beyond just providing you with the theory, with 30+ activities that have been used to train and coach thousands of salespeople globally, in companies such as Meta, Google, Salesforce, Snowflake and Experian.

With contributions from more than 20 thought leaders, who share their experiences, challenges and stories, the book stands as a comprehensive resource for any salesperson wanting to build a successful and sustainable career.

About the Author

Hi, I'm **Chris Hatfield**, Founder and Coach at Sales Psyche. I've spent the last 15 years in several sales, leadership and coaching roles, and I have always had a passion for supporting people in unlocking their potential and creating a healthier mind. I'm a qualified Coach (Advanced Certificate in Coaching Practice: accredited by the Association for Coaching) and have worked with companies such as Meta, Google, Experian, Salesforce and Virgin Media/O2, to name a few.

My interest in the mind stemmed from my own personal experience of struggling with my mental health and mindset, particularly with anxiety. When I started out in sales, doing door-to-door selling on 100% commission, it came to be a real crippling experience, and my anxiety would often cause me to withdraw and struggle to perform.

But I didn't want this to define me or limit me, so I started to seek a better understanding of where it stemmed from and how to build a healthier relationship with my mind and self-talk. Our inner dialogue can be our greatest strength, but also our biggest threat. I began to learn how it could serve, rather than sabotage, me.

I saw throughout my sales career that this topic wasn't properly understood, rarely talked about, and if it was, it was a very reactive conversation. This is why I started my company, Sales Psyche. I support those in the sales world with their mindset and mental wellbeing, to normalise the conversation. I work to assure people that they're not alone in how they think or feel, and to equip them with the tools to be proactive in taking care of their mind. This was one of the biggest drivers for me writing this guide.

I also focus on Attachment Theory as a coach, and you may see me pop up on your TikTok feed (chris_hatfield) sharing content and tips on working on this.

Outside of my work I love keeping active, and have always seen that as a big part of taking care of my own mind. Running has become my latest go-to, and the community it brings with it has given me a new sense of fulfilment in my life. I'm fascinated by history and regularly listen to podcasts focused on this. And, I'm learning Italian, which has been a great experience to go back to a beginner's mindset with.